R-2330-MRAL

November 1979

Labor Substitution in the Military Environment: Implications for Enlisted Force Management

Mark J. Albrecht

A Report prepared for

OFFICE OF THE ASSISTANT SECRETARY OF DEFENSE/ MANPOWER, RESERVE AFFAIRS AND LOGISTICS

PROLOGUE

Since the completion of this research in mid-1978, the national debate on the need to modify the general terms of national military service has focused on many alternatives, including consideration of a return to conscription. Although the author neither endorses nor dissents from this potential change in public policy, a comment may be appropriate on how the research findings presented here relate to military manpower costs and effectiveness in the context of a draft environment. In an analytic determination of the efficient mix of first term and career personnel, the three key inputs most sensitive to a draft are first term labor costs, productivity, and supply.

Since none of the current proposals for a return to military conscription include provisions for reverting to the discriminatory first term pay policies of the pre-All-Volunteer Force (AVF) era, it is reasonable to assume that the relative wage data included in this analysis will remain valid regardless of the mode of military service adopted.

Although no firm evidence exists on the impact of mode of service on performance, it is also reasonable to assume that first term draftees would be no more productive than their volunteer counterparts.

The impact on first term labor supply deriving from draft legislation would be to expand that supply substantially at relatively constant marginal budget costs. For the purposes of this analysis, however, no limit to first term labor supply at current relative wage rates has been imposed. The rationale for this approach is discussed in the text, but the key here is that a reversion to the draft would have no impact on the analytic results.

In sum, the cost and the effectiveness of military manpower resources are and will remain matters of serious national concern. Consequently, methods for estimating the least costly combination of manpower resources at acceptable levels of effectiveness, and the policies implemented to achieve those combinations, will be important to defense manpower planners. Thus, this analytic work, begun in the context of an all-volunteer force, is germane for conscripted force planning and should be considered in any overall plan for change.

M. J. Albrecht
Falls Church, Virginia

PREFACE

This report was prepared as part of Rand's Manpower, Mobilization, and Readiness Program, sponsored by the Office of the Assistant Secretary of Defense/Manpower, Reserve Affairs, and Logistics—OASD(MRA&L). The study was conducted under Task Order 78-V-3, First Term/Career Substitutions.

With manpower issues assuming an ever greater importance in defense planning and budgeting, the purpose of this studies program is to develop broad strategies and specific solutions for dealing with present and future defense manpower problems. This includes the development of new methodologies for examining broad classes of manpower problems, as well as specific problem-oriented research. In addition to providing an analysis of current and future manpower issues, it is hoped that this studies program will contribute to a better general understanding of the manpower problems confronting the Department of Defense.

Perhaps the most urgent policy imperative arising from the tremendous increase in military manpower costs over the past decade is to enhance efficiency through improved personnel policies. In this regard, military manpower policy decisions have come to be regarded as falling as much in the area of resource allocation as in that of personnel management. Within the set of manpower resource allocation questions, none is more important than the distribution of personnel by length of service, frequently described as the mix of first-term and career personnel.

The present report addresses the problem of enhancing the ability of defense manpower planners to determine efficient allocations of manpower resources by length of service, focusing on the measurement and evaluation of labor productivity in the military environment.

The report has also been submitted and accepted as a doctoral dissertation as partial fulfillment of the requirements of the Ph.D. for the Rand Graduate Institute.

SUMMARY

The determination of desirable mixes of first term and career enlisted military personnel and the implementation of policies designed to achieve these mixes have long been regarded as two important management objectives for defense manpower planners. The enlisted experience mix is a significant factor in force cost and capability and, given the closed nature of the military personnel system, in the key personnel issues of grade structure and promotion opportunity. Until recently, the desirability of alternative mixes of enlisted manpower resources has been influenced more by considerations of personnel management than resource management. However, with the tremendous increase in military manpower and personnel costs over the last decade, attention has shifted to considerations of economic efficiency in the allocation of these resources.

This report considers the economically efficient allocation of military manpower resources by length of service—in particular, the supply and demand conditions of seventeen specific Air Force occupational specialties. The research was conducted to analyze the potential for cost savings associated with the substitution of first term and career personnel at the occupational level. Its analysis of the measurement and evaluation of labor productivity in the military environment makes it possible to assess the potential for making first term/career substitutions.

An efficient mix of first term and career enlisted personnel will either minimize total force costs at a specified level of effectiveness or maximize effectiveness for a given total cost. In theory, these mixes are achieved when the marginal costs of first term and career personnel just offset their marginal contribution to military effectiveness. The difficulty with making these determinations derives from an inability to accurately assess the relative productivity and substitutability of various categories of military labor.

The Enlisted Utilization Survey (EUS) data base, a unique data base recently assembled at Rand, permits a detailed evaluation of the question of relative productivity and substitutability of first term and career personnel in the context of different military occupational specialties. For this research, productivity measures and work unit background data from the EUS data base were used to estimate the parameters of a two-tiered constant elasticity of substitution (CES) labor aggregation function for a number of military occupations. This CES formulation can provide estimates of the relative productivity of first term and career personnel over all possible input combinations. In addition, it explicitly allows for the fact that the relative productivity of first term and career personnel will likely change with changes in the overall experience mix. The specific magnitudes of changes reflected in the function are empirically derived and hence minimize the role of analytic assumption in the specification of the aggregation function.

Estimated labor aggregation functions can be placed in the context of a simple optimizing framework using current marginal cost and supply information to provide estimates of the economically efficient mix of first term and career personnel differentiated by occupation. Such an optimization analysis is conducted using a marginal costing approach. A supply function based on past empirical research on the relationship between enhanced first term retention and career wage is used to reflect the constraint on enlisted career supply in the optimization analysis.

The research findings indicate that the potential for substitution between first term and career labor within particular occupations is significant but limited. The elasticity of substitution between first term and career personnel within particular occupations is neither zero, which would indicate no substitution potential, nor infinite, which would indicate an unlimited substitution potential. Additionally, the analytic results substantiate the intuitive premise that productivity is positively related to experience and that the substitution potential and the relative productivity of experience categories are both related to occupational skill level. We found that more technically demanding occupations tend to be associated with lower first term productivity relative to career productivity, reflecting the length of time required to become job skill proficient in the first term, as well as with lower elasticities of substitution, indicating the necessity of maintaining a relatively fixed career proportion of the work force.

The CES formulation of the military labor aggregation function is shown to be both a useful and reasonable reflection of actual production. Specifically, the findings indicate that the CES formulation is superior to either of the two most commonly used formulations, the linear aggregation function and the Cobb-Douglass formulation.

The policy recommendations that follow from the productivity analysis concern an expansion of current service capabilities for determining production alternatives either by exploring technically feasible combinations experimentally or by using current variations in production to indicate feasible alternatives. This capability could be expanded either by research initiatives or by expanding the role of organizations devoted to determining requirements within the services to include not only the determination of manning levels and manhour requirements by occupation or mission but also a determination of alternative manpower configurations at different overall manning levels and with different manhour requirements.

The significance and utility of the productivity estimates presented in this research have been demonstrated in the context of optimization analyses conducted for each of the occupations in the sample. The findings of the optimization analyses indicate that for the sample of occupations included in the study, the current overall mix of first term and career personnel falls within the range that one would select on the basis of economic efficiency alone. However, although the distribution of personnel for the sample of specialties taken in the aggregate is consistent with cost effectiveness considerations, the distributions within specific occupations are not. Specifically, the results of the analysis indicate that, in general, higher skill occupations tend to overutilize first term labor inputs and lower skill occupations tend to underutilize them. This result underscores the importance of conducting force structure analyses at the occupational level. The differences between the current distributions within the set of occupations included in the study and the implied efficient distributions have important cost consequences: A redistribution of existing first term and career personnel within the set of occupations analyzed would mean almost a $20 million annual cost savings, with no loss in overall effectiveness.

Unlike the comparison between the actual distribution and the implied efficient distribution, a comparison between the implied efficient distribution of enlisted personnel by occupation and the objective foce distribution by occupation set by the Air Force as force structure goals, reveals substantial differences. Cost considerations aside, the findings of this research suggest that the attainment of objective force goals would be associated with a substantial reduction in overall effectiveness. The analysis shows that the objective force structure proposed by the Air Force may not be technically feasible at current effectiveness levels. Thus, whatever benefits that might be associated with moving to the objective force will be offset by reductions in actual capabilities.

From a policy perspective, the findings of the optimization analysis indicate that a redistribution of manpower resources toward a more senior force in high skill occupations and toward a major junior force in lower skill occupations would be cost effective, despite the fact that reenlistment bonuses may be required to retain additional career personnel in high skill occupations. In fact, this research indicates where reenlistment bonuses could be more efficiently used. More importantly, the objective force structure for the Air Force varies substantially from what appears to be the economically efficient distribution of enlisted personnel by length of service with the consequence that overall effectiveness may decline.

The role of the Office of the Secretary of Defense (OSD) in the determination process should be one of providing guidance and incentives to each of the services for making economically efficient allocations of manpower resources. OSD cannot make such determinations for the services, nor should it adopt that position. What can be done, however, is to demonstrate general approaches and methodologies to the service with respect to the determination of important resource allocation problems and to pursue the guidance with specific incentives for expanding current capabilities in this regard.

ACKNOWLEDGMENTS

The author wishes to extend thanks to the many individuals who have made this research possible.

First, the author gratefully acknowledges Richard V. L. Cooper, director of Rand's Manpower, Mobilization, and Readiness Program. His continued support and guidance throughout the author's tenure at the Rand Graduate Institute have contributed substantially to this report.

Special thanks are due, likewise, to other members of the program, especially Robert M. Gay, whose collaboration on the development and administration of the Enlisted Utilization Survey proved to be an invaluable asset in the development of this research. The author has also benefited from the many useful comments and criticisms of Rand colleagues Glen Gotz and David Chu, and from the programming assistance of Pat Gowen and Dolph Hatch. Furthermore, the author acknowledges the useful comments of S. Chapel and J. DaVanzo on an earlier draft.

For their continued support and comments on earlier drafts of the report, the author wishes to acknowledge Major Ralph Praeger (USAF) and Major Michael Bryant (USA) of the Military Personnel Policy Division of the Office of the Assistant Secretary of Defense, Manpower, Reserve Affairs, and Logistics.

Finally, as this research represents the author's doctoral dissertation at the Rand Graduate Institute, special thanks are due to dissertation committee members James Foster and Professor Robert M. Solow of the Massachusetts Institute of Technology. Most importantly, the author wishes to acknowledge the contribution of dissertation chairman C. Robert Roll, Jr. His encouragement and assistance throughout the conduct of the research far exceeded what any doctoral student could reasonably hope to enjoy. Naturally, any errors or omissions that remain are the author's sole responsibility.

CONTENTS

TABLES

FIGURES

I. INTRODUCTION

> In a civilized society, soldiers are maintained altogether by the labour of those who are not soldiers, and hence the number (and quality) of the former can never exceed what the latter can maintain over and above maintaining both themselves and the other officers of government they are obliged to maintain.
>
> Adam Smith, *The Wealth of Nations*

An important allocation decision facing military manpower planners is the distribution of enlisted personnel by length of service—a distribution that affects not only total force cost and capability but also, given the closed nature of the military personnel system, force management in terms of grade structure and promotion opportunity. This report can aid defense decisionmakers in allocating manpower resources economically and efficiently, as well as in evaluating and measuring labor productivity in the military environment.

Selecting and implementing a policy to attain "desirable" distributions of enlisted personnel by length of service has long been a major manpower planning issue confronting defense manpower officials. Historically, the "desirability" of such distributions has hinged more on personnel considerations than on concerns of cost effectiveness.[1] This emphasis was a natural by-product of the draft era when the supply of enlistments was relatively unconstrained and the cost of junior personnel was extremely low. At the same time, however, the Services were experiencing problems of large personnel "humps" (unusually large numbers of personnel with the same amount of service) stemming from accession policies during the Korean War, and large "valleys" (unusually small numbers of personnel in the same experience category). These humps and valleys made a consistent promotion pattern and hence, a career pattern impossible to guarantee.

Under these conditions it was reasonable for the Services to focus on the management implications of the force mix. As a result, in the late sixties a great deal of effort was devoted to developing management policies to provide distribu-

---

[1] The need to establish a "desirable" enlisted force was first brought into focus during the late fifties when the Cordiner Committee requested the Services to submit the first term reenlistment rates required to sustain a desirable career content. The Department of Defense subsequently requested the Services to review alternative force structures and establish objectives that would guide management programs and assist in evaluating progress.

Early initiatives appear to have been begun in 1959 with a comprehensive study by the Air Force entitled the "Optimum Career Airman Force Program." Analyses of the subject were also conducted by other Services throughout the years immediately prior to the conflict in Southeast Asia. A 1963 Army study directive calls for the development of "the optimum content of the Army in regard to its makeup of inductees, first-term enlisted personnel, and career soliders, with the view of developing long range objectives which will provide positive guidance to all concerned with the procurement, management, and retention of enlisted personnel." In essence, a similar task was given to the Services by the Office of the Secretary of Defense (OSD) in 1968, when guidance was issued for the development of long range enlisted force management systems. The Air Force response to the OSD requirement, the Total Objective Plan for Career Airman Personnel (TOPCAP), was approved in 1971. Similar long range plans for the other Services have now been approved and are updated annually. I am indebted to Major M. Bryant, MRA&L(MPP), for providing this background information.

tions of personnel that would minimize the potential for management problems like those experienced in the late 1950s and early 1960s.[2]

With the advent of the All-Volunteer Force (AVF) and the substantial increases in pay for enlistees, the problems of total force cost and capability became prominent manpower planning concerns. Consider that in 1964, generally regarded as the last pre-Vietnam year, manpower and personnel costs were just over $25 billion, slightly less than 40 percent of Department of Defense expenditures. But in 1977 those costs had exceeded $60 billion and were almost 60 percent of DOD's total budget. At that time the absolute size of the active force had declined by over 13 percent. One reason manpower costs rose so dramatically after the move to the AVF was DOD's lack of response to the changing cost and supply conditions of the enlisted force.

Table 1 compares the average monthly basic pay for first term and career personnel for selected years from 1958 to 1973. Table 2 shows the distribution of personnel by length of service, for selected years from 1966 to 1977. Prior to the Vietnam era, the pay of enlisted personnel with less than four years of service was slightly less than 50 percent of that of personnel with five or more years of service. At the same time, first term personnel accounted for almost 60 percent of the entire enlisted force. More recently, however, first term wages have risen to almost 65 percent of career wages; yet service-wide, first term enlistees are still almost 60 percent of the enlisted force. This suggests that although first term personnel are now both more expensive and less plentiful, the Services have not incorporated these factors into "desirable" distributions of enlisted personnel.

Although it has received some analytic attention, the complex problem of determining economically efficient allocations of manpower resources remains one of the major unresolved questions in the management of the All-Volunteer Force.[3] The issue is difficult to address for three reasons:

1. The distribution of personnel by length of service, or the experience mix of the force, is inextricably bound to other important policy questions such as mobilization, readiness, youthfulness and vitality of the force, reserve supply, and deployment strategy. Thus, distributions that are cost effective in a narrowly determined economic context may not necessarily be desirable in the overall context of defense objectives.
2. The structure of the military labor market is unique. Basically, the closed nature of the military personnel system and its lengthy service contracts make the estimation of both labor cost and supply extremely difficult. This means that to minimize costs in an economic framework a great deal must be known about the productivity of individuals over time who are now, or who may be, members of the military service.
3. It is difficult to define precisely what defense output is and hence to measure how various military inputs contribute to it. In the case of military

---

[2] The Air Force in 1971 instituted the first models for personnel management, TOPCAP (enlisted) and TOPLINE (officer). Shortly thereafter, the Navy designed and implemented the ADSTAP personnel planning model. All three of these models are designed to provide a "smooth" force profile around a minimum career requirement. For a detailed analysis of these and other personnel models, see Jaquette et al. (1977).

[3] The major research efforts in this regard are Smith (1964), Fisher (1970), and Jaquette and Nelson (1974). The continuing undertaking of the basic allocation problem is addressed in Cooper (1977).

Table 1

COMPARISONS OF MONTHLY BASIC PAY FOR FIRST-TERMER AND CAREER PERSONNEL

Year	Average Monthly Basic Pay		Career/First-Term Pay Ratio
	First-Term	Career	
1958	$118	$247	2.09
1964	141	288	2.04
1968	175	373	2.13
1971[b]	246	490	1.99
1973	365	563	1.54

[a]Weighted average of basic pay for first-termers (<4 years) and careerists ($\geq$4 years); calculations based on (1) FY1972 pay grade distribution for each year of service, and (2) Service objective plans for year-of-service distributions (furnished by OASD (M&RA)).

[b]Before the AVF pay raise.

Table 2

PERCENTAGE OF THE ENLISTED FORCE IN THE FIRST TERM

Fiscal Year	Army	Navy	USMC	USAF	DOD
1962	66	61	66	46	59
1964	66	61	66	46	59
1966	74	64	74	50	65
1968	81	67	82	55	72
1970	80	67	80	50	69
1972	65	62	75	50	61
1974	64	57	73	51	59
1976[a]	64	58	74	47	59
1977[b]	63	58	74	46	59
Force Obj.	63	57	73	57	61

SOURCE: Data furnished by OASD (M&RA).

[a]As of September 30, 1976.

[b]As of September 30, 1977.

manpower resources, the problem is to assess the relative productivity of various types of labor.

The research reported here provides empirical estimates of both the relative productivity and the substitutability of first term and career personnel using a sample of occupational specialties in the Air Force enlisted force.

Section II presents a general framework of analysis for determining economically efficient allocations of manpower resources by length of service, focusing on the first term/career mix, and the specific methodology adopted for this analysis. Section III analyzes the problem of measuring enlisted productivity in the military environment, and Section IV describes the Enlisted Utilization Survey (EUS) data base, which provides the basis for empirical estimation of labor productivity for a number of Air Force occupational specialties. The productivity measures included in the EUS data base are examined in Section V, which focuses on the relative productivity and substitutability of first term and career manpower resources. Estimates of labor aggregation functions serve to summarize the productivity and unit composition data for each of the occupations in the sample. Section VI provides an illustrative optimization framework for determining economically efficient allocations of first term and career manpower resources, using the labor aggregation functions estimated from the EUS data set. Section VII presents the conclusions, research extensions, and policy recommendations. Appendixes A and B give additional details about the EUS survey, and Appendix C discusses the basic costing method described in Section V.

II. GENERAL FRAMEWORK AND METHODOLOGY

When viewed strictly in terms of resource allocation, the optimal distribution of enlisted personnel by length of service would (1) minimize total force costs at a given level of military effectiveness or (2) maximize effectiveness at a given level of cost. This section presents a general framework for evaluating the economic efficiency of first term and career enlisted manpower resource allocation alternatives, the specific information requirements of the determination process, and the particular cost and productivity contexts adopted for this analysis.

SCOPE

This analysis uses the basic technique of *suboptimization* where the objective is to minimize the cost of providing a given level of military effectiveness by substituting experienced, trained personnel (members of the career force) for inexperienced, untrained personnel (members of the first term force).[1] This analysis attempts to find policies that when applied to a small part of the total national security problem will provide the best use of resources devoted to that part. Of necessity such an approach takes many important resource allocation questions as given; consequently, results of this analysis will likely be sensitive to higher order allocation decisions. If current distributions change, the results may change also.[2]

Military effectiveness is the end product of combining labor, land, and capital to form and train military units and activities. These units and activities may or may not actually conduct military operations; their effectiveness in peacetime results principally from their potential to conduct military operations.

The problem of measuring effectiveness is a difficult one and not unlike measuring personal well-being. There are no satisfactory units. There is no such thing as too much—only too little. More is always better than less, but more must always be acquired at either a higher cost or by enhanced effficiency. Even though we cannot measure military effectiveness directly, we can measure the manpower inputs to it. A central part of this analysis, of course, is that not all military personnel contribute equally to military effectiveness. Thus, using relative productivity measures, we can take a specified total enlisted force distributed by occupational specialty and convert total numbers of personnel in each specialty to effective equivalents.

We seek cost effective mixes of first term and career personnel that will minimize the present value of the cost stream incurred in providing a specified present value of effective man years of service to specific occupational specialties, assuming that the net result of all other influences on military effectiveness remains unchanged.

Some important restrictions to this analysis should be stated at the outset. First, the analysis is limited to a set of seventeen Air Force occupational specialties

---

[1] Hitch (1953) provides a rigorous definition of suboptimization and its limitations.

[2] Much of the formulation of the general framework of the analysis is drawn from Smith (1964).

whose personnel in aggregate constitute only slightly more than 25 percent of the Air Force enlisted force; even taken by aggregate measures, the sample is not exhaustive. The occupational specialties included in the sample, however, represent a wide range of technical difficulty, including highly skilled occupations such as avionic electronics repairs as well as rather low level skills such as food preparation and supply specialties. Because of this wide range and the similarities among occupational skill types within the sample, the analysis of a subset of occupations will be meaningful in evaluating the efficiency of allocations for all others in the Air Force.

A second restriction concerns time streams and present values. For purposes of this analysis the transition costs of force restructure are largely ignored. That is to say, this research compares steady-state forces rather than the present values of each of the alternative forces. As mentioned before, dynamic considerations are important because changes in the enlisted force structure cannot be achieved immediately; in many cases they would require more than twenty years. However, because we want to assess the potential for cost reduction or effectiveness gains associated with a reduced reliance on a predominantly junior force, our approach underestimates the savings associated with a move to a more senior force. The benefits associated with reduced demand for new recruits will be enjoyed almost immediately while many costs associated with an increase in career personnel will not be borne for a number of years.

Because of these limitations, the results of this research do not constitute and are not intended to serve as strictly determined sets of local optima for the first term/career mixes. Rather, they suggest feasible spaces of force restructure consistent with cost effectiveness considerations and suggest directions for change *given the current enlisted force structure.*

GENERAL FRAMEWORK

Development of a general framework of the analysis hinges on the distinction between first term and career personnel. This is the key to analyzing the problem of a cost effective experience mix of the enlisted force. Essentially, the analysis specifies the consequences, in terms of both costs and returns, of a reenlistment decision at the end of the first term of enlistment. These consequences, properly stated, shed light on the cost effective mix for a specific occupational specialty by estimating the maximum number of career personnel to retain before it becomes more efficient to acquire new enlistees.

The general framework within which the current suboptimization procedure is carried out derives from the economic theory of the firm. The fundamental concept is that of a cost minimizing firm which can substitute between two inputs (first term personnel and career personnel) to achieve a given level of output. Asssociated with each of these two inputs is an expected value of effective man years and an expected cost. In general, the least costly force of any given effectiveness will result when the incremental contribution to effectiveness of first term personnel and of career personnel just balances the incremental cost of hiring an additional member of each category.

This relationship can be summarized by the equation:

$$\frac{MP_c}{MC_c} = \frac{MP_f}{MC_f} \tag{1}$$

where MP_c = marginal productivity of career personnel,
$\quad\;\; MP_f$ = marginal productivity of first term personnel,
$\quad\;\; MC_c$ = marginal cost of career personnel,
$\quad\;\; MC_f$ = marginal cost of first term personnel.

As mentioned previously, a key element of this analysis derives from our expectation that the costs and productivities of first term and career personnel will be quite different. For example, we would expect that the marginal product of a career member, MP_c, will generally exceed the marginal product of a first termer, MP_f, for several reasons. The career member is more effective than the first termer because more investment has been made in training the careerist and in giving him on-the-job experience. Furthermore, career personnel are available to contribute fully to effectiveness throughout a term of service, whereas first term personnel must have at least basic military training and, in most cases, some form of advanced training before they can effectively enter the force. Hence for any specialty i, it is likely that, on average,

$$MP_{ci} > MP_{fi} \tag{2}$$

Similarly, because career personnel occupy higher pay grades, have greater pay seniority,. and are much more likely to qualify for a retirement benefit,

$$MC_{ci} > MC_{fi} \tag{3}$$

That is, in general, one input is both more expensive and more productive than the other. To find the efficient mix of personnel for any given occupational specialty, we need an optimization framework for assessing the relative costs and benefits of first term and career personnel simultaneously over a wide range of force mix alternatives.

The general design of such an optimization framework for the military force mix problem has been provided by Jaquette and Nelson (1974) and later elaborated on by Munch (1977). In both of these studies specific cost and supply models reflecting the military compensation system and closed personnel system were derived from actual cost data and empirical research regarding labor supply in the military context. However, in neither case were actual productivity data used to specify the productivity relationships between different types of military labor. Although using the same general framework for the optimization analysis, the present research focuses on the estimation of productivity relationships using productivity data. The basic elements of the optimization framework are described in Section VI. The general productivity model adopted for this analysis, its characteristics, and its utility for the force mix problem are discussed below.

In our development of conditions of economic efficiency, we stated that the relative values of first term and career marginal productivity depend not only on the experience of the two groups, but also on the specific mix of the force. Clearly, adequate specifications of the general model in terms of productivity for each occupation must include two key elements: (1) measures of the relative productivity of first term and career personnel and (2) some measure of how these relative productivities change with changes in the input mix.

As a first step in specifying the requirement of the general model in terms of productivity we will want a reformulation of the efficiency conditions in terms of productivity alone. This can easily be accomplished by rearranging terms of the general efficiency conditions expressed in Eq. (1). Rearranging terms in (1) we find that all other things being equal, the conditions of economic efficiency can be likewise expressed as

$$\frac{MP_{ci}}{MP_{fi}} = \frac{MC_{ci}}{MC_{fi}} \tag{4}$$

and interpreted as an equation of the ratio of the marginal products of two inputs and the ratio of their marginal costs. This formulation is more useful analytically since it recasts the general efficiency conditions in terms of costs and productivity alone, and thus allows us to address each issue independently, at least initially.

With regard to productivity, the formulation of efficiency conditions in Eq. (4) is a particularly useful one since it can be interpreted directly in the context of the economic theory of production. Assuming that substitution between first term and career personnel is possible within a given occupation, the first term in (4) indicates the tradeoff potential between first term and career personnel which at a specific output level will leave that output or effectiveness level unchanged. This term corresponds to the economic concept of the marginal rate of substitution between factors of production at one particular production point, a useful measure for specifying overall production processes. Thus, the initial requirement from the general model that productivity be expressed in terms of the marginal productivities of first term and career personnel can now be defined in terms of the marginal rate of substitution between first term and career labor at particular production points. Furthermore, the general model's assertion—that the ratios of productivity to cost will tend to equilibrate given substitution between the two labor types—can now be reformulated in terms of productivity alone, namely that changes in the first term/career mix will affect the marginal rate of substitution.

In a sense, this latter condition indicates the ease of substitution between first term and career inputs. That is, the less responsive the marginal rate of substitution is to changes in the mix, the broader the ranges of substitution opportunity, and conversely, the more the rate of substitution changes, the narrower the substitution opportunity.

For an accurate assessment of production efficiencies, we must specify how dissimilar manpower inputs are to be translated into military effectiveness. The economic concept of a production function provides one method of aggregating inputs based on their relative productivity and substitutability and relating these aggregate measures to levels of output. In theory, production functions are defined for all inputs to the production process; however, within the context of suboptimization, parts of the overall production function may be specified contingent on some assumptions about the nature of the production function as a whole.

For a given level of military production or effectiveness, we can conceive of many different combinations of inputs that will achieve that level efficiently. With respect to manpower inputs, we can think of a specific level of military production that will represent the maximum achievable output for either a small, relatively experienced labor force or a large, relatively less experienced one. We can think, therefore, of an explicit functional relationship between the effectiveness levels and labor inputs that reflects these conditions.

Consider the aggregate effectiveness function,

$$E = f(Z, L_f, L_c), \tag{5}$$

where E is a measure of military effectiveness, L_f represents first term labor inputs, L_c represents career labor inputs, and Z represents all other inputs to military effectiveness. The expression of effectiveness levels in terms of first term and career labor inputs alone is based on the assumption that it is legitimate to rewrite (5) as

$$E = F[Z, f(L_f, L_c)] = f(Z, L^*). \tag{6}$$

We then seek the proper specification of the function

$$L^* = f(L_f, L_c), \tag{7}$$

where L^* is the total supply of fully effective personnel equivalent to military effectiveness.

The concept of a labor aggregation function is based on the assumption that the effectiveness function (5) is separable in the form of (6). The requirements of separability are stringent, namely that the levels of nonlabor inputs (Z) have no influence on the relative marginal productivities of different types of labor inputs.[3] Thus, for this analysis, we have obscured the possibility of differences in the degree of complementarity between nonlabor inputs and various types of labor.

Returning to the aggregation function defined in (6), the rate at which we can exchange first term for career labor inputs at the margin, while holding effectiveness constant, reflects the marginal productivities of the two types of labor at that point. These substitutions, however, may not be direct in the sense of two raw recruits doing the exact work of one experienced individual.

For example, consider the case of a specific avionics repair shop operating with 5 experienced technicians and 10 inexperienced trainees. At this manning level, reducing the experienced group by 1 man may be offset by the addition of 3 more inexperienced trainees. Together these trainees will not accomplish the exact same tasks as the experienced technician but will, in all likelihood, be assigned to many different tasks requiring little or no experience. Thus the remaining experienced technicians will have more time to accomplish the tasks requiring more advanced technical skills. At that particular manning level we can think of a 3 to 1 tradeoff of inexperienced for experienced personnel while holding output, or effectiveness, constant.

Now the avionics repair shop operates at the same effectiveness level, but manned by 4 experienced technicians and 13 inexperienced trainees. But at this new manning level, a reduction of the experienced group by 1 technician may not be adequately offset by 3 additional trainees. As many as 5 trainees may be required to replace 1 experienced man in the indirect manner we described before.

---

[3] For a thorough and formal discussion of these functional relationships and their implications see Leontief (1947).

At the new manning level, the tradeoff of inexperienced for experienced labor is 5 to 1. This underscores the need for first term/career productivity assessments to include not only the marginal rates of substitution between input types reflected by relative marginal productivities, but also some indication of how these rates change given changes in the overall mix.

One measure that explicitly reflects changes in substitution opportunities associated with changes in the input mix is the elasticity of substitution. This measure represents the proportionate rate of change in the experience mix divided by the proportionate rate of change of the tradeoff opportunity, that is, the marginal rate of substitution. Mathematically, the elasticity of substitution between first term and career inputs from (6) can be expressed

$$\frac{d \log \frac{L_c}{L_f}}{d \log \left(\frac{\partial E}{\partial L_f} \Big/ \frac{\partial E}{\partial L_c} \right)} \tag{8}$$

The labor aggregation function used as a specification in this analysis is the constant elasticity of substitution (CES) function first introduced by Arrow, Chenery, Minhas, and Solow in 1961.[4] Mathematically, this function has the property of allowing any positive value for the elasticity of substitution between inputs, and although initially designed for two inputs—capital and labor—can accommodate any number of inputs as long as the elasticity of substitution between any pair is constant over all ranges of inputs. The general form of the function is

$$E = (a \, X_1^{-\rho} + (1 - a) \, X_2^{-\rho})^{-\frac{1}{\rho}}, \tag{9}$$

where the parameter $0 < a < 1$.

The marginal productivities of the inputs in this formulation are

$$\frac{\partial E}{\partial X_1} = a \left(\frac{E}{X_1} \right)^{\rho+1} , \quad \frac{\partial E}{\partial X_2} = (1 - a)\left(\frac{E}{X_2} \right)^{\rho+1} , \tag{10}$$

the marginal substitution is

$$\text{MRS} = \frac{a}{1 - a} \left(\frac{X_2}{X_1} \right)^{\rho+1} , \tag{11}$$

[4] Arrow et al. (1966).

and the elasticity of substitution is

$$\sigma = \frac{1}{1 + \rho} \, . \tag{12}$$

Thus the parameter ρ is closely related to the elasticity of substitution and hence is referred to as the substitution parameter of the function.

The α's are distribution parameters. They reflect the relative productivity of the different inputs. For example, if $\alpha = 1 - \alpha$, then the marginal productivity of first term and career personnel is equal at the point where the number of first term and career personnel is equal.

The CES function therefore includes the special cases of infinite elasticity and zero elasticity, since from (12) when $\rho = \infty$, $\sigma = 0$; and when $\rho = -1$, $\sigma = \infty$. The proof of the latter is trivial. The former requires a complicated limiting argument.[5]

The usefulness of this particular function as a specification of production processes derives from its previously mentioned flexibility and analytic tractability. Reformulating (7) in terms of the ratio of the marginal products of first term and career personnel, we see that

$$\frac{MP_f}{MP_c} = \frac{a_c}{a_f} \left(\frac{L_c}{L_f} \right)^{\rho+1} , \tag{13}$$

and taking logarithms of both sides of the equation, the parameters may be directly estimated by ordinary least squares (OLS) regression. This shows how the first term-career ratio for a particular occupation changes with changes in the ratio of the productivities of the two labor inputs.

Use of this particular functional form for an analysis of labor aggregation is not unique. In his study of the role of education in economic growth, Samuel Bowles (1970) first used the CES function to estimate the elasticity of substitution among labor types with different levels of education across occupations. Following a similar approach, Dougherty (1971) used the CES formulation to specify a labor aggregation function that used occupation as opposed to education as a basis of disaggregating labor types. In both of these cases, international cross sectional data were utilized for estimating relationships between marginal products and input ratios, and in both cases wages were used as proxy measures for marginal productivity. The results of these two analyses indicated that the manpower requirements approach to education planning (essentially a fixed factor production function) should be abandoned, but that the elasticities of substitution among occupational labor types were sufficiently high to be adequately approximated by an infinite elasticity of substitution model.

The present analysis, although analogous in approach, is quite different in terms of scope because it addresses the substitution of experience categories within *specific* occupations rather than across *different* occupations.

---

[5] For the formal proof see Henderson and Quandt (1971, p. 87).

The specific CES function proposed for this analysis is a nested constant elasticity of substitution function of the general form:[6]

$$E_i = \left[a_1 \, L^*_{fi}{}^{-\rho_i} + a_2 \, L_{ci}{}^{-\rho} \right]^{-\frac{1}{\rho_i}} \tag{14}$$

and

$$L^*_{fi} = \left[\sum_{i=1}^{n} a_i \, L_{fji}{}^{-\theta_i} \right]^{-\frac{1}{\theta}} , \tag{15}$$

where

$$\sum_{i=1}^{n} a_i = a_1 + a_2 = 1$$

$$-1 < \rho_i = \frac{1 - \sigma_i}{\sigma_i} < \infty \qquad i = 1, \ldots, n$$

$$-1 < \theta_i = \frac{1 - \sigma_j}{\sigma_j} < \infty$$

Overall specialty effectiveness, E_i, is a CES function in a first term labor index (L^*_{fi}) and career labor (L_{ei}). L^*_{fi}, in turn, is a CES function in actual first term inputs (L_{fji}). To illustrate the application of this function to a specific occupation, the L_{fji} may denote the set of first term inputs within which individuals are perfect substitutes, i.e., year of service. L^*_{fi} denotes the number of quality-adjusted equivalents in the first term of service, and L_{ci} denotes the number of career equivalents. The two-tier formulation permits variation in the elasticity of substitution between pairs of basic inputs. Thus, it can be specified that men in different year groups within the first term are better substitutes for each other than men in the career force. In the limit, men in a first term of service for a specific occupation are perfect substitutes for one another, and (15) reduces to

$$L^*_{fi} = \sum_{i=1}^{N} a_i L_{fji} , \tag{16}$$

where a_i is the marginal productivity of first term personnel in the ith year of a first term of service.

---

[6] This extension of the basic CES formulation was first described in Sato (1967).

The reason this nested or first tier function has been included in the general formulation follows from our earlier discussion of the general formulation of the experience mix allocation problem. We argued then that the first term-career distinction was a useful, but admittedly arbitrary, disaggregation of military manpower resources. The formulation of a nested CES function allows us to address the issue of nonhomogeneity among first term inputs and to test the hypothesis that a linear aggregation of first term inputs is in all cases the appropriate specification of the first term labor index.

III. PRODUCTIVITY MEASUREMENT

This section discusses the general problem of definition and measurement of labor productivity in the military environment. Various measurement techniques are evaluated, with emphasis on their attributes and applicability as a potential data base for providing estimates of (1) the marginal rate of substitution and (2) elasticity of substitution between first term and career personnel.

PROPERTIES OF PRODUCTIVITY MEASUREMENT FOR AN ANALYSIS OF THE ENLISTED EXPERIENCE MIX

In this section the advantages and disadvantages of alternative approaches to the measurement problem are assessed for their conceptual appropriateness and the applicability of resulting data to the problem of estimating military productivity.

Productivity measures to evaluate the consequences of the utilization of additional first term or career personnel should (1) measure net marginal productivity rather than gross marginal productivity; (2) be linked to the personal characteristics of the individual to whom they apply; and (3) be linked to the unit composition within which the members of the sample work.

First, the relevant productivity measure in determining an efficient mix of enlisted personnel by length of service is net marginal productivity, that is, the increment to military effectiveness that can be attributed to an additional reenlistment or replacement. It is important to distinquish *net* from *gross*, or *direct*, productivity. The two are not necessarily the same and are often confused. As we use the terms, an individual's *gross* marginal productivity is the amount he personally contributes to unit effectiveness; his *net* marginal productivity is the net difference between the unit's effectiveness level in his presence or absence. The two need not be the same, and the relationship between them can be expected to change systematically with experience.

Consider, for example, a new recruit joining a work unit just after completing his advanced training. Initially, he will be able to complete some simple tasks, but he will almost certainly need fairly close supervision. His gross marginal productivity under these circumstances would be represented by the work he personally completes. However, the decline in his supervisor's production above and beyond the necessary supervisory responsibilities of routine unit management represents a real decline in potential unit effectiveness; thus the new recruit's net marginal productivity will represent the net difference between the two manning levels. As the recruit acquires more experience, his gross marginal productivity will normally increase, and the amount of direct supervision he requires will decrease. As a result, net marginal productivity rises more rapidly than gross marginal productivity. At some point, direct supervision will become minimal, and gross and net marginal productivity will, for all intents and purposes, be identical.

To the extent that the two measures do differ, however, net marginal productivity is clearly the relevant concept because it measures the impact on actual mission effectiveness associated with the utilization of additional personnel. Furthermore, for estimates of first term productivity, these differences are likely to be quite large and will substantially affect an analysis of the relative productivities and cost effectiveness of first term and career personnel. Productivity estimates that measure gross or direct marginal productivity rather than net marginal productivity will tend to overstate the initial productivity of enlisted personnel, hence implying efficient mixes that would use excessive first term manpower resources. Thus, the case for using measures of net marginal, as opposed to gross marginal, productivity derives not only from conceptual reasons, but more importantly, from the differences in results the two approaches provide.

Productivity measures should also permit estimates to be made with respect to specific individuals and those estimates to be related to the personal characteristics of those observed. As previously mentioned, the distinction of military labor by terms of service is an admittedly arbitrary, but useful way of categorizing enlisted personnel. It is likely, however, that these categorizations of experience may classify essentially nonhomogeneous labor inputs together, especially during the first term of service. To determine homogeneous first term subgroups for the purpose of making productivity analysis of labor category more accurate, we must be able to assess the productivity of a variety of subgroups within the first term category independently. Because relative productivity will likely change dramatically within a first term, more accurate estimates of average first term productivity can be derived from subgroup estimates than from overall estimates of the first term average.[1] Thus, productivity measures should be made with respect to specific individuals and, in turn, these measures related to the characteristics of the individuals observed.

Finally, measures of individual productivity should be linked to the particular experience mix and manning level of the work unit from which they are drawn, since determining an efficient mix of manpower resources depends not only on knowledge about the relative productivities of specific experience groups but also on how these productivities are likely to change with changes in the overall mix. In a sense, then, the particular experience mix of an individual's work unit represents a microcosm of the entire enlisted experience mix. Since the experience mix is likely to vary from unit to unit, measures of relative productivity that can be related to unit composition will allow us to evaluate the productivity of specific experience categories over a wide range of labor force environments.

ALTERNATIVE MEASUREMENT PROCEDURES AND EXAMPLES IN THE MILITARY CONTEXT

Measures with the properties described above can be gathered in a number of ways. This section describes the strengths and weaknesses of three major alternatives and how each applies to the problem of estimating military productivity.

Effectiveness Measurement

The general character of the productivity measures one would collect with unlimited resources is fairly straightforward. It would involve estimating an indi-

---

[1] The reasons for this assumption will be more fully developed later.

vidual's net productivity by measuring a unit's effectiveness in his presence and absence. For example, a particular unit's effectiveness or output could be measured with its full complement of personnel and then with various combinations of n – 1 personnel. Then the difference in effectiveness with and without a given person would be the measure of his net contribution to unit effectiveness.

The basic problem with this approach, however, is that measuring military effectiveness is extremely difficult. As previously mentioned, military effectiveness defies parameterization; no unit of measure across occupations is satisfactory. As a result, this approach is most applicable where there are proxy measures of output or effectiveness such as direct production of some service or output such as radios repaired or maintainence achieved, etc. However, even within the context of tangible output, measuring unit output is difficult to do.

Even within a given occupation, there are many different types of output. Within a given shop, for example, several types of equipment may be maintained and repaired and many types of failures may occur. If the difficulty of repairing different types of failures over time varies substantially, the number of repairs that can be turned out in a given number of man-hours will vary substantially. Weights must be developed for different types of repair, and output must be measured as a weighted sum of the type of repairs accomplished. When the context is broadened to include multiple shops, the development of appropriate weights is even more important because of differences in equipment mixes among shops.

It should be apparent from the preceding discussion that the "ideal" sort of productivity measures would be quite costly to assemble and would, in spite of the cost, be less than perfect. However, several attempts have been made to use effectiveness measurement to assess productivity in the military context.

Two notable instances of the direct measurement approach are Scifers (1974) and Horowitz and Sherman (1976). In the former study, the measure of output selected reflected the number of direct maintenance man-hours attributable to the number and type of avionics repairs accomplished by several avionics repair shops in the Air Force. The measure was selected not only because of its proximate relationship with actual output, but also because it is a standard Air Force accounting measure for assessing workloads and designing maintainence schedules.

Horowitz and Sherman used a measure of failure rates among specific types and classes of naval vessels as proxy measures of output for naval missions. Again this measure was selected on the basis of its relationship to output and the availability of data as a standard accounting metric. In both cases the number of observations were of necessity extremely limited and the problems of controlling for intervening variables were substantial. The problem in avionics repair estimates concerned adequate control for workload surges and dissimilarity of repair type, as well as the inherent bias in the estimates stemming from the fact that they are self-appraisals used for performance evaluation. In the case of ship failures, maintenance history and specific conditions of sea duty make measures of system failure difficult to interpret in the context of manning levels alone.

Job Knowledge Tests

One approach that retains the characteristics of direct measurement but involves measures that are simpler to develop and administer is the *job performance testing approach*. This concept involves testing individuals on a specific set of skills used in their specialty. By testing people with different amounts of on-the-job experience, or one person at several points in time, the relationship between productivity and experience can be estimated.

There are several major limitations to this approach, however. It involves measurement of direct or gross marginal productivity rather than net marginal productivity, and there are real questions about how well such tests measure productivity. Even if the *set* of job tasks accurately reflects the duties in a particular occupation, they may not be a good reflection of a particular individual's actual duties, and hence his real contribution to unit effectiveness.

In addition, job tests administered in a controlled environment will not provide insight into how actual job performance relates to the specific work unit's composition. Thus, even though two individuals perform identical on-the-job tests, their individual contribution to unit effectiveness may differ depending on how the work in their particular unit is organized and what manpower resources the unit has to accomplish its mission.

Job knowledge tests have been used to evaluate military productivity, as in the Project Utility Study conducted by the Human Resources Research Organization of the Department of the Army (Vineberg and Taylor, 1972). In this study, the performance of enlisted specialists in four Army occupations (armor crewman, general vehicle repairman, supply specialist, and food management) were evaluated using objectively scored job sample tests involving representative tasks taken from each job. The results of these tests were plotted against the months on the job of those observed to provide a performance profile for each occupation in terms of on-the-job experience. The sample included over 350 observations per occupation. The results of the research indicated, among other things, that performance is positively correlated with experience, and that performance does not tend to decline at any time before twenty years of service.

Problems with this kind of measure derive from important time and cost constraints actual measurement imposed on the sample size (in this case only four occupations were analyzed), as well as from the uncertain relationship between performance as evidenced by job knowledge tests and actual on-the-job productivity; that is, the difference between an individual's *potential* for performance and his *actual* on-the-job performance. Furthermore, this particular case implicitly assumes that the scale of performance is identical to the scale of actual productivity. For example, since the specific job tests were unweighted in terms of performance scores, there is an implicit assumption that a 1 percent difference in performance scores corresponds to a 1 percent difference in actual productivity. Since, however, it is unlikely that all job tasks in a given occupation contribute equally to unit effectiveness, such measures will tend to misrepresent real on-the-job productivity depending on the relationship between the two scales and the relevant job task weights. Finally, even if these job knowledge scores actually did reflect productivity, they would reflect measures of gross marginal, as opposed to net marginal, productivity. They would thus tend to systematically overestimate the productivity of individuals early in a service career.

Supervisory Ratings

The most common approach to assessing the productivity of military personnel involves the use of supervisory ratings of productivity rather than direct measurement of productivity. Although this approach has the disadvantage of providing subjective measures of productivity, it has many advantages, especially since lower costs of collection allow for substantial increases in sample sizes and for more precise distinctions between military occupations.

Regardless of the survey technique used (mail questionnaire, interviews, etc.), the inherent subjectivity of supervisory ratings is likely to be aggravated by definitional problems. For example, the definition of relevant criteria for productivity, or the relevant sample population, each contributes to the level of "noise" or unexplained variation in resulting productivity estimates. This is not to say that these measures are not useful, but simply that a great deal of care must be taken in designing and interpreting specific rating schemes. Furthermore, the fact that productivity estimates derived from supervisory rating techniques allow for many different specific methodologies and behavioral assumptions indicates that our ability to make direct and precise comparisons of derived measures across data sets will be very limited. Many attempts have been made, however, to estimate military productivity through the use of various rating schemes. Although the validity of each set is specific to the particular issue at hand in some way, examples of two approaches are discussed below in some detail.

Data Set for the Defense Study Group on Military Compensation. In the first example of data derived from ratings techniques, supervisory estimates of the time required for trainees to achieve journeyman status are exhibited. Relative productivity is inferred from the averages of these estimates by tracing out a time path of productivity. One data set using this approach was derived from a 1963 questionnaire for the Defense Study Group on Military Compensation (DSGMC). Enlisted supervisors answered questions regarding the number of months after completion of training required for the average specialist to become fully effective at the apprentice, journeyman, and supervisor skills levels. Their responses were plotted with skill level on the vertical axis and time in months on the horizontal axis. Values of relative productivity for year of service were interpolated by averaging over the year in question. The responses were tabulated for 22 specialties, ranging from highly technical to low skill occupations. All service specialties were classified into 22 groups on the basis of which most nearly corresponded to the skill requirements of the 22 measurements available. These assessments were made on the basis of the occupational specialty manuals of each service.

Observed responses were used to discriminate between 22 broad groupings; no discrimination on the basis of this learning curve measure was made within these groups. This treatment makes the learning curve a very blunt instrument for the separation of specialties, but at least allows for some occupational discrimination of productivity.

Clearly the broad scope of this particular data set introduces a series of validity considerations that transcend the basic problem of subjectivity bias in supervisory ratings. First, the measures reflected in the 1963 DSGMC survey represent a supervisor's estimates of the learning curve of the "typical trainee." Previous research has indicated that productivity estimates for the "typical trainee" are not necessarily equivalent averages over all trainees. This research suggests that in evaluating the typical trainee, supervisors tend to give too little weight to outliers in the distribution, especially those few individuals who required substantially more on-the-job training than the average to attain a reasonable level of proficiency (Gay, 1974). Thus, there is some reason to be concerned that this particular exercise might provide upward biased estimates of the true relative productivity of the average specialist.

An additional concern stems from the broad classification of first term personnel by occupation. A surveyed supervisor was asked to evaluate the "typical trainee" in one of the 22 broad occupational categories he felt qualified to evaluate; in many cases a supervisor rated two or three occupational categories. What results are not only extremely broad occupational categories but also inadequately controlled cognizance of supervisors for rendering a useful judgment on particular occupation types. That is to say, there was no mechanism to relate the supervisor's occupation to the occupation or occupations he specifically rated. Thus, for example, a senior enlisted electronics repair specialist may have provided not only an estimate of the learning rate of the typical field radio repairman, but also of the rate of an automotive repairman or cook. This brings into question the validity of the estimates in terms of breadth of occupational distinction as admitted by the DSGMC, as well as the validity of the productivity estimates themselves within occupational categories.

Finally, although the DSGMC acknowledged that the inherent subjectivity bias in the ratings data was important, it made no attempt to systematically control for the effect. Related research has demonstrated that unless this effect is controlled, serious errors in the estimates are likely (Cooper and Nelson, 1976). The purpose of this critique is not to denigrate the DSGMC but to suggest the problems likely to arise from productivity data derived through this and similar techniques.

Data Set for ADSTAP. Another example of a data set derived from ratings techniques was assembled by B-K Dynamics for the Navy as an input to the naval personnel planning model, ADSTAP. It employs rating schemes that use direct evaluations of productivity rather than evaluations inferred from estimates of the time required to become proficient at specific job tasks. In the case of the B-K Dynamics (1973) work, supervisors were asked to rate the *utility* to the Navy of specific enlisted pay grades at different lengths of service.

In its final form the utility data set consists of estimates of the utility of the average enlisted man in each pay grade over thirty years of service. The estimates were derived from a series of Delphi questionnaires administered to a panel of 75 senior enlisted personnel serving in the Second Fleet of the Navy. The Delphi participants were asked to assess the initial utility to the Navy of the Direct Procurement Petty Officer at pay grades E-2 through E-9 as proxy measures of the value of the average enlisted man at entrance to the service. Midpoints on the utility curves were estimated by averaging participants' estimates of the year of service when an enlisted man in each pay grade reaches maximum value to the Navy, and the length of time the average man who remains in each pay grade for thirty years of service will maintain his maximum value. Finally, participants were asked to assess the value of the average man in each pay grade at the end of thirty years.

Although the inherent subjectivity biases of the respondents were controlled for by an application of the iterative Delphi methodology, the specific form of the Delphi experiment raises some general questions of validity. The first involves defining the productivity measure. In the B-K Dynamics research, the concept selected to reflect productivity was *utility*, defined as a measure of value relating to the general good of the Navy. Such an ambiguous definition is likely to generate a great deal of error in the data because the participant's ratings may apply to a wide range of concepts, only a few of which may relate directly to the concept intended by the analysts.

Another problem involves determining the relevant population for description. As previously noted, the concept of the typical or average trainee—even when perfectly related to a subpopulation, say, individuals with four years of experience—is likely to generate biased estimates due to the behavioral tendency to underestimate outlying marginal performers. In the B-K Dynamics work, however, the relevant population is based on pay grade subcategorized by length of service. The concept of, say, an average E-3 with thirty years of experience is difficult to interpret. Does "average" in this case refer to the hypothetical average E-3 evaluated at the thirty year point, or the average E-3 who in fact does remain an E-3 for thirty years? Such ambiguity adds confusion to the resulting estimates.

In general, attempts to estimate military productivity by using rating techniques that employ direct estimation complicate the inherent problem of reliability and validity. Subjective bias in the data is caused by problems of definition and comprehension of the measure elicited.

Conclusions. To summarize, subjective measures of productivity, although advantageous in terms of cost and sample size, are also extremely difficult to deal with analytically. Inherent bias is associated with the subjective nature of the measures, proper classification of occupations, definitions of the relevant population, and definition and comprehension of the measures elicited. All of this is not to say that such measures are useless, but rather that they create additional burdens of uncertainty and must be carefully designed and interpreted.

A data set selected for the current analysis is described in Section IV, including its design and administration, the characteristics of the assembled data set, estimates of its limitations, and finally an assessment of its utility for an analysis of military effectiveness as outlined in Section II.

IV. THE ENLISTED UTILIZATION SURVEY (EUS)
DATA BASE [1]

A large and, in many respects, unique data base was recently asembled at The Rand Corporation to analyze how different amounts of first term specialty training affect net training costs. This section describes the Enlisted Utilization Survey (EUS) data set collected between January and February 1975 under contract funds provided by the Defense Advanced Research Projects Agency. The specific research for which these data were generated concerned the optimal mix of formal school training and on-the-job training for a variety of miliary occupational specialties, with emphasis on an assessement of the efficient amount of technical training for specific specialties. The specific approach adopted involved estimating the costs of formal training (faculty and student salaries, supplies, etc.) and its benefits (i.e., improvement in a trainee's on-the-job performance) to determine how training variations affected net training costs. This was the primary consideration in the design and administration of the Enlisted Utilization Survey.

The actual data collection design involved four major steps.

1. Selecting a set of specialties to be included in the study.
2. Identifying individuals serving in one of the selected specialties who appeared to be in their first term of service and serving at their first duty station. Service personnel files were used for this purpose.
3. Sending these individuals a mail survey designed with three basic objectives: identification of the trainee's primary supervisors; verification of his suitability for inclusion in the study; and collection of background information not included in the service record.

Identification of the individual's supervisors was the key element of the initial survey. A mailing list was made up and survey forms constructed to survey supervisors for ratings of the trainees. The mailing list for each military unit with responding trainees contained (1) the name of each supervisor who was identified by a responding trainee and (2) the names of all trainees who identified that individual as one of their supervisors. A copy of the supervisor survey form was then compiled for each supervisor named and a rating sheet included for each individual who had named the supervisor. Thus, the supervisor survey instrument's length varied depending on the number of trainees under his supervision.

The specific supervisor survey form contained three parts: (1) questions about the general conduct of on-the-job training in the unit and an explanation of the productivity concept used in the survey; (2) a set of questions about the utilization, performance, and attitudes of the specific trainees who had named the supervisor; (3) a section in which the supervisor was asked to rate a "typical trainee" at various points of a first term of service.

These are the basic mechanics of the Enlisted Utilization Survey. The characteristics of the trainee and supervisory surveys, and the specific form of the productivity measure used in this research, are described further below. The dis-

---

[1] See Appendix A for a further description of the EUS.

cussion applies to samples from the Army, Navy, and Air Force included in the survey, but for purposes of the actual productivity analysis we restrict our consideration of the data base to the set of Air Force occupational specialties.

TRAINEE SURVEY

The initial survey of the EUS was designed primarily to identify supervisors of those individuals who, from data in the service personnel files, were shown to be first term personnel serving at their first duty station. Two secondary purposes of the survey were to verify the respondent's suitability for inclusion in the sample by virtue of military occupation and service status and to obtain certain background and attitudinal information on the individuals that was not available from the service personnel files. This section briefly describes the survey instrument that was developed to accomplish these objectives, the process by which individuals were selected for inclusion in the sample, response rates to the survey, and measures of representativeness of the obtained sample.

The trainee questionnaire form was developed between January and October 1974.

Sample of Individuals

The overriding consideration in selecting individuals for inclusion in the initial sample was that they be in the first term of service and that they be serving at their first duty station. The determination of which individuals were serving at their first duty station was made by an analysis of the service personnel files. In general, all individuals in a specialty selected for inclusion in the study who appeared to be in a first term of service and serving at their first duty station were surveyed.

In a few large specialties where there were 1000 or more such individuals, a clustered random sample was drawn, with the clusters based on unit of assignment. Cluster sampling was done to improve the quality of the estimates of productivity being collected. As previously noted, one factor affecting the estimation of a given individual's productivity is the way the person doing the rating tends to rate individuals in general. Methods of controlling for this potential bias include multiple ratings made for specific individuals or multiple ratings made by a single supervisor. In either case cluster sampling by concentrating within units will render more applicable approaches to control for this kind of bias.

Survey Administration

The survey of trainees was conducted from November 1974 through January 1975. All mailings were made to trainees at the duty address shown on the personnel files, and because of the sequential nature of the total survey process, only trainees stationed in the continental United States were included. Persons whose responses had already been received were not included in the subsequent mailings.

As Table 3 shows, over 30,000 trainees were surveyed. The overall response rate of 65.4 percent is quite respectable for a mail survey. These response rates were computed by taking responses as a percentage of delivered questionnaires (that is, subtracting the undeliverable mail from the initial mailings to form the

Table 3

TRAINEE SURVEY RESPONSE

Service	Number Mailed	Number Undeliverable	Percent Undeliverable	Number Returned	Response Rate
Army	10,679	1,329	12.4	5,142	55.0
Navy	9,588	597	6.2	6,558	72.9
Air Force	11,422	890	7.8	7,173	68.1
Total	31,689	2,816	8.9	18,873	65.4

denominator). The rationale for estimating response rates in this way is, of course, that individuals who do not receive a questionnaire cannot be expected to respond.

Representativeness of Respondents

The individuals in the sample to be analyzed (i.e., those responding to the questionnaire) should be representative of all first term personnel in the specialties. Table 4 shows the relationship between members of the initial sample and survey respondents on several important personal characteristics. Each entry represents the percentage of the relevant group with that particular characteristic. For example, the table indicates that 3.9 percent of all Air Force personnel originally surveyed were in mental category I. While there were some differences between the respondents and the total sample, these differences are generally quite small. Thus, while respondents and nonrespondents may differ on attributes for which we have no measures, there seems to be little basis for concern about the nonrepresentativeness of respondents based on the measures that are available.

SUPERVISOR SURVEY

The collection of productivity estimates from supervisors identified in the survey of the trainees was the most important single aspect of the EUS data collection efforts. Because subjective estimates of military productivity are extremely sensitive to the design and implementation of specific survey instruments, it is worthwhile to explore the supervisor survey in some detail.

Instrument Development

The supervisory survey form was developed over the course of about seven months (January-July 1973) through a series of visits to military installations. Field work on the supervisor survey instrument was continued until there was a high degree of correspondence between written and verbal responses.

Questionnaire Format

The final questionnaire consisted of three sections. The first contained questions

Table 4

COMPARISON OF TOTAL SAMPLE AND RESPONDENTS

Personal Characteristic	Army		Navy		Air Force	
	Total Sample	Respondents	Total Sample	Respondents	Total Sample	Respondents
Mental Category						
I	2.9	3.7	9.3	9.3	3.9	4.6
II	28.7	32.7	47.7	47.8	36.1	38.4
III	52.9	50.7	41.7	41.5	58.1	55.3
IV	15.4	12.9	1.5	1.5	1.8	1.7
Civilian Education						
Non-high School Graduate	30.3	25.4	22.2	21.0	5.6	4.4
High School Graduate	52.9	56.8	54.2	55.3	78.4	79.9
GED[b]	8.8	8.4	5.3	4.8	8.2	6.8
Some College	7.0	8.1	16.8	17.6	5.2	6.1
College Graduate or More	1.0	1.4	1.3	1.3	2.6	2.6
Race						
White	65.7	65.3	66.3	64.4	70.0	69.0
Black	32.8	33.1	32.1	34.1	28.5	29.7
Other	1.5	1.6	1.6	1.5	1.5	1.3
Sex						
Male	93.3	91.8	94.0	93.7	90.1	89.9
Female	6.7	8.2	6.0	6.3	9.9	10.1
Marital Status						
Single	65.7	65.3	66.3	64.4	70.0	69.0
Married	32.8	33.1	32.1	34.1	28.5	29.7
Other	1.5	1.6	1.5	1.6	1.5	1.3
Age						
17–18	7.8	5.4	5.8	4.4	6.2	4.3
19	24.1	22.9	17.0	17.0	33.3	31.5
20	24.1	24.3	16.4	17.6	25.8	27.1
21	18.7	19.6	15.8	16.1	15.8	16.9
22	12.7	13.5	14.3	14.0	8.5	9.1
23–24	8.1	9.4	18.0	18.0	7.2	7.6
Pay Grade						
E-1	2.4	2.1	.7	.7	3.7	2.5
E-2	28.4	25.8	21.2	20.8	33.4	31.2
E-3	31.9	32.2	32.1	32.6	59.6	62.3
E-4	33.5	35.1	28.6	28.5	3.3	4.0
E-5	3.8	4.1	16.5	16.4		
E-6			.9	1.0		

[a]Column totals may not sum to 100 due to rounding errors.

[b]Certificate of General Education Development--i.e., high school equivalence.

dealing with the way on-the-job training was conducted, and the way trained personnel were used in the respondent's unit. The second section had two parts: (1) a description of the concept of productivity elicited, along with a simple test of comprehension; (2) a set of questions about a specific individual who named the respondent as one of his supervisors. The total length of the questionnaire depended on the number of trainees who said that they were supervised by the respondent. The third section dealt with the productivity of the typical trainee, both technical school graduates and direct duty assignees.

Productivity Measures

Productivity is a complex phenomenon that can be measured in a number of ways. The guidelines used in developing productivity measures for the Enlisted Utilization Survey, and the ways in which these objectives were incorporated into the final survey instrument, are described below.

A pilot study conducted before this research began indicated that useful measures of productivity could be developed for mail administration and also that through refinements and modifications more accurate estimates were possible. In addition to being capable of administration by mail, the measures should be useful in a variety of types of specialties, be relatable to the personal characteristics of the individuals observed, and measure net or marginal productivity as opposed to direct or gross productivity.

The survey instrument was to be administered by mail so that a large number of individuals could be surveyed. The difficulty of measuring productivity and the fact that little measurement has been done in the military context meant that there were sure to be questions regarding the validity of the estimates made in the survey and very little to compare the estimates with. The usefulness of the data could be assessed by evaluating the pattern of results in a wide variety of circumstances.

The measures developed focus on the first four years of military service, which usually coincide with the first term of enlistment for most enlisted personnel. Unless they change specialties, individuals with four years of service have essentially achieved journeyman proficiency, and although their job skills can be expected to improve somewhat with further experience, they will not be learning a substantial number of new, skill-related tasks after that point. Thus the data focus on a period of service when job tasks are most homogeneous across individuals and when most individuals are almost exclusively involved with skill-related job tasks.

The need for an estimating method that is useful in a variety of occupations is obvious. Since the training study required cross service comparisons, an instrument that could not be used in one or more occupations would have imposed severe limitations on the scope of the research. If separate methods of estimating productivity had to be developed for each set of job tasks, the research would have been limited in two ways. First, the added costs of instrument development would have limited the number of specialties that could have been included, and, second, the lack of cross specialty uniformity would have eliminated one important basis for evaluating the usefulness of the estimates.

Relating productivity estimates to the personal characteristics of those observed is important because the characteristics of individuals will likely have an important impact on performance. The ability to relate personal characteristics to job performance in many varied specialties offers real potential for assessing the relationship between experience and productivity and, hence, the cost effectiveness of particular experience mixes.

Finally, a major consideration in developing measures of productivity was that they measure net rather than gross productivity. Gross productivity measures an individual's *direct output* while net productivity measures the *change in total output* asssociated with an individual's presence. For a trained individual the two are virtually the same, but that is not true of an individual early in a service career. Such an individual's gross productivity is generally substantially greater than his net productivity. During on-the-job training more resources than would be required for a trained individual tend to be devoted to direct supervision and instruction for the trainee. Since these resources could, in the absence of the trainee, be devoted to current production, *unit* output suffers from their use in the OJT process. Net productivity, by focusing on unit output, is designed to allow for both the trainee's direct contribution to unit effectiveness and his indirect reduction of effectiveness. Using measures of gross productivity to appraise the value to the military of various experience categories would, through inflated estimates of early on-the-job performance, result in upward biased estimates on the initial value of military personnel, which in turn would lead to overestimates of the cost effectiveness of inexperienced personnel.

Many survey instruments were tested during the instrument development phase of the research, and in each case an effort was made to ensure that they satisfied the criteria just described. In addition, the instrument development profited from an earlier pilot study which indicated that useful measures of net productivity could be obtained through a mail survey of enlisted supervisors.

Figure 1 shows the rating scale that formed the basis of the research approach for productivity estimation. This set of questions was asked about each trainee who had responded to the trainee survey. Four points in the individual's first term of service were chosen—his first month on the job, the time at which the rating *was* completed, one year from that time, and after four years of service.[2] At one month of service the individual's net productivity was assumed to be lowest, his direct productivity at a minimum, and the amount of time required from those who worked with him at a maximum. To construct a complete profile, this point would have to be estimated directly or indirectly; direct estimation should be more reliable. Similarly, four years of service was included as the upper limit on first term productivity. The time of the rating was used because it is the single point for which the best estimate is possible and, in fact, it is this data point that was selected for analysis of productivity in the current context of first term/career substitutions. More will be said about this later in the discussion of our use of this data set.

The standard of reference for these ratings is the "average specialist with four years of experience." By almost any definition this would be a journeyman specialist who requires no more than routine supervision. This rating system provides a common frame of reference that can be used in any specialty.

Supervisors were asked to estimate net productivity by the individual's direct contribution to unit production minus the foregone productivity of persons who directly supervise and instruct him. This measure captures the most important difference between gross and net productivity—the foregone productivity of super-

---

[2] By associating the return date of the questionnaire with the data from the individual's personnel file showing the date he joined the unit, a length of experience associated with the two intermediate points was established.

5. We would like you to estimate this individual's *NET CONTRIBUTION TO UNIT PRODUCTION* at several points in his service career *assuming he serves 4 years or more in this shop or section.* An individual's *NET CONTRIBUTION TO UNIT PRODUCTION* is his direct production *minus* production lost by others who supervise and instruct him.

Relative to the average specialist with four years experience, how would you rate this individual's *NET CONTRIBUTION TO UNIT PRODUCTION:*

A. During his FIRST MONTH with your unit? (CIRCLE ONE DOT—DOTS ARE AT 5% INTERVALS)

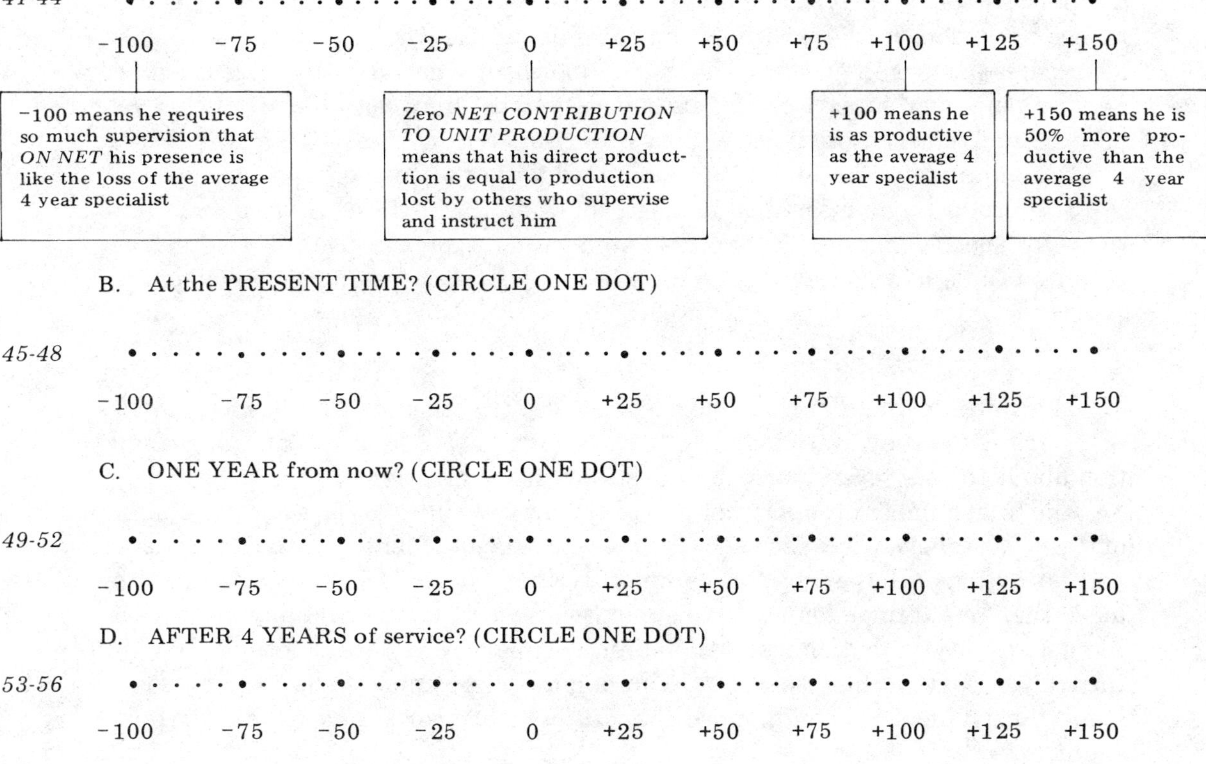

Fig. 1—Productivity rating scale

visors—but it does ignore some other, less important differences. Specifically, it does not include resources devoted to additional record keeping that may be done for new trainees, correspondence or special field-conducted training courses, etc. But data collection, field work, and previous empirical work have shown that these are small costs relative to the costs for the additional supervision trainees receive. The scale ranges from - 100 percent to +150 percent, where the former means that the individual requires so much supervision that having him with the unit is equivalent to the loss of a specialist with four years of experience and the latter that he is 50 percent more productive than the typical four-year specialist. While the range does not necessarily encompass all the possible actual values of productivity found among members of the sample, it seems safe to assume that values outside the range occur quite infrequently.

Another productivity estimate included in the study relates to rating the performance of "typical trainees." These ratings provide a way of estimating the average performance of individuals in a given specialty and of controlling for differences among supervisors in terms of their system of rating productivity. How a supervisor rates the typical individual says something not only about the performance of persons in that specialty, but also about the way that particular supervisor rates persons in general. That is, a supervisor who rates the typical trainee lower than other supervisors in his specialty rate him can be expected to rate specific individuals more harshly than other supervisors. This information can be used to eliminate some of the bias associated with a supervisor's system of rating.

The productivity measures included for the typical trainees were similar to those for specific individuals, and the same rating scale was used. The four basic points in time, however, were one month, one year, two years, and four years.

Survey Administration

The Initial mailing of the supervisor survey, to a list created from responses to the trainee survey, was made in early February 1975. Table 5 contains information about the survey response by questionnaire and rating.

The total number of supervisor forms mailed was almost as large as the number of trainees surveyed because each trainee was asked to identify three supervisors, and on average, they identified about 2.5. Many supervisors were identified by more than one trainee (on average supervisors were named by 1.5 trainees), and the net result was that almost 30,000 unique supervisors were identified. As with the trainee survey, the response rate among those presumed to have received the survey instrument was high, more than 70 percent overall and in the Air Force slightly less.

The percentage of mail returned as undeliverable was about twice as high as for the trainee survey for two reasons. First the addresses used in the supervisor forms were based on trainees' identifications. Misspellings of names or incorrect designations of rank probably caused some mail to be undeliverable. Second, the supervisors' addresses were less current than the trainees'. Although the personnel tapes from which the trainee mailing addresses were taken had been updated two to four weeks before the first mailing, almost three months elapsed between the time the first trainee surveys were received and the first supervisor surveys were mailed. Transfers of personnel during this period also contributed to the higher rate of undeliverable mail.

Table 5

SUPERVISORY SURVEY RESPONSE

Service	Response by Questionnaire					Response by Rating					
	(1) Number Mailed	(2) Number Undeliv- erable	(3) Percent Undeliv- erable	(4) Number Re- turned	(5) Response Rate[a]	(6) Number Mailed	(7) Ratings per Question- naire Mailed[b]	(8) Number Undeliv- erable	(9) Ratings per Undeliv- erable[c]	(10) Number Re- turned	(11) Ratings per Question- naire Returned[d]
Army	7,665	1,940	25.3	3,897	68.1	11,606	1.51	2,324	1.20	6,246	1.60
Navy	10,834	1,408	13.0	7,110	75.4	15,663	1.45	1,684	1.20	10,396	1.46
Air Force	11,048	2,007	18.2	6,254	69.2	18,150	1.64	2,984	1.49	10,679	1.71
Total	29,547	5,355	18.1	17,261	71.4	45,419	1.54	6,992	1.31	27,231	1.58

[a]Col. 4 ÷ (Col. 1 – Col. 2).

[b]Average number of trainee rating forms in the questionnaires mailed out. Col. 6 ÷ Col. 1.

[c]Average number of trainee rating forms in the questionnaires that were returned by the post office. Col. 8 ÷ Col. 2.

[d]Average number of trainee rating forms in the questionnaires returned by respondents. Col. 1 ÷ Col. 4.

The average number of trainees included in the undeliverable mail (Table 5, Col. 9) was uniformly lower than the average number in the initial supervisor mailing (Col. 7). Since one can reasonably assume that the number of trainees supervised is at least partially dependent on rank, one can assume that more junior than senior addresses were not located. However, the average number of ratings per returned questionnaire (Col. 11) was very similar to the average number of ratings per questionnaire mailed.[3]

A number of important limitations of the productivity data should be considered. First, the concept of net or marginal productivity is fairly sophisticated. It is not one that enlisted supervisors are likely to have been familiar with prior to the administration of the survey. This raises the possibility that some survey responses will be invalid because supervisors did not understand what they were being asked to do. Recognizing this possibility, a simple test of comprehension was included in the survey instrument (see Appendix B). Clearly, some responses cannot be used because the rater did not understand the concept of net productivity, but a preliminary analysis of the data does not indicate that this was a serious problem.

Another important limitation of the productivity data is the difference among raters in their rating systems—some tend to rate easy and others hard: some tend to see people as very similar and some as very different. This has the potential for producing substantial noise in the data, and the pilot study indicated that it was indeed a serious consideration. For this reason supervisors' estimates of the productivity of the "typical trainee" were included in the survey as a basis for controlling for this kind of bias. The specific manner of control, however, is extremely important for a detailed analysis of productivity based on this data set.

Finally, the data set consists of estimates of the productivity of first term personnel made relative to the fully qualified specialist in that occupation. Thus, the data set includes *actual* productivity data for first term personnel only. For the purposes of this analysis we have assumed long term enlisted productivity to remain constant after a first term of service. This assumption is not unprecedented in analysis of the enlisted mix issue, but is sufficiently important to discuss in some detail.

With respect to the likely bias introduced into the analysis by making this assumption, the evidence is ambiguous. On one hand it is reasonable to assume that an individual's contribution to unit effectiveness will tend to increase beyond the first four years of service. On the other hand, however, it is also likely that during a 20- or 30-year career there will be periods—in some cases quite long periods—when productivity will likely decline. These periods might be associated with PCS moves and job changes, overseas rotation, or simple job boredom. On net, however, it seems reasonable to assume that productvity will tend to increase beyond a first term of service. The extent of this increase and hence the average value of career personnel are uncertain, but they are clearly understated by invoking the assumption of constant productivity. Nevertheless, to the extent that bias is introduced into the analysis by assuming long term productivity to remain constant, this bias works in the direction of understating career productivity and hence in overstating the cost effectiveness of first term personnel.

The productivity estimates derived from the Enlisted Utilization Survey are made for first term personnel alone, and they are indirect, subjective estimates of

---

[3] All of the numbers shown here are raw returns prior to data cleaning.

productivity rather than direct measures of production. These limitations should be kept in mind in the interpretation of the analytic results.

INTEGRATED DATA BASE

As previously mentioned, to be useful for specifying the productivity requirements of the general model, a data set needs to (1) reflect marginal productivity, (2) be related to specific individuals whose personal characteristics are known, and (3) be related to the unit composition of the specific work units from which the sample is drawn. We have shown that the EUS satisfied the first two of these requirements and have suggested its potential with respect to the third. In this subsection the organization of the integrated data base—which includes both productivity estimates from the EUS and unit characteristics drawn from the service personnel files—will be discussed, as well as some general characteristics to the data set with respect to unit composition.

The unit characteristic data were integrated with actual productivity estimates from the EUS by accessing the service personnel files and matching each specialty code and unit identifier on the trainee files with the specialty codes and unit identifier of all enlisted personnel included in the personnel files. All personnel records that matched unit and specialty codes with the codes on the trainee sample were then extracted from the full personnel file. This extract was surveyed by specialty and unit code to categorize enlisted personnel by length of service and mental category. Thus, for each specialty/unit combination, a string of categorized data was compiled which summarized unit composition in terms of length of service and mental category. Since this procedure required access to the entire service personnel file and since the only service personnel file made available in entirety for the training study was the Air Force personnel file, the integrated data set and hence this analysis of the EUS data set are limited to the Air Force sample. The analysis could be expanded to include the Army and Navy sample of the EUS data base with additional data.

In its final form each observation assembled in the data base consists of a supervisory rating of a specific individual, the personal characteristics of the individual observed, the supervisor's rating of the "typical trainee," and categorized data regarding the specific composition of the work unit from which the observation was drawn. At this point it will be useful to examine some general characteristics of the sample in terms of unit composition, both to determine the feasibility of the analytic approach and to suggest the potential for implementing changes in the experience mix at the unit level.

Sample Characteristics

The overall analytic approach and methodology adopted for this analysis were based, at least in part, on the assumption that variations in unit composition within a specialty existed and that these variations would provide a basis for determining the relationship between marginal rates of substitution and the experience mix. Thus, the first important consideration with respect to the general character of the data set regards the existence of variations in the experience mix across units for specific occupations. From a purely technical point of view, the absence of variation in experience mixes across sampled units would make it impossible to estimate the proposed productivity model. More generally, since a lack of variation in the unit composition might derive either from sampling errors or a real lack of variation in the entire population of units, it would be impossible to discriminate between the hypothesis that the potential for substitution exists but is not reflected in the sample, and the hypothesis that substitution is in fact impossible. In any respect, a lack of variation in unit composition in the sample would provide a rather strong argument for the infeasibility of such substitutions in reproducing reality, regardless of the technical possibilities stemming from organizational constraints at the base level.

Tables 6 and 7 display two examples of the distribution of first term/career ratios by units included in the sample: the cryptographic repair specialty (306X0) and the aerospace ground equipment repair specialty (421X3). The tables show the frequency of occurrence of units having first term/career ratios between 0 and 5 to 1 in increments of 0.1. In both cases there is a great deal of variation in unit composition and the distributions have a generally normal shape. In the case of the cryptographic repair occupation, the mean of the distribution is 1.42 to 1 first termers to careerists per unit. For the aerospace ground equipment repair specialty the mean ratio is 2.30 to 1. This is consistent with what we would have expected a priori. Since the cryptographic repair occupation is more technical, we would expect to find more technically demanding occupations associated with lower first term/career ratios in terms of unit composition.

Distributions constructed for each of the sampled occupations exhibit similar patterns of variations in unit first term/career ratios, indicating that there is sufficient variation in the data to provide estimates of the productivity relationships entailed in the general productivity model. Furthermore, the existence of substantial variation in the first term/career ratio in the sample indicates that substitution potentials do exist in these occupations.

Another important element of the unit data is the average size of the units observed, which provides an additional check that the units represented in the sample accurately reflect the units in the population. Although this factor is difficult to assess with any real precision because it is not easy to rigorously determine what the typical unit size for an occupation is, some broad generalizations can be made. Some notions of the typical unit size for each of the sampled occupations were obtained from field work associated with the selection of specialties for the taining study and the criterion of potential sample size. These admittedly non-rigorous estimates, however, match fairly well with the general characteristics of the sample and thus suggest that the sample is likely to be fairly representative of the populations as a whole.

Table 8 summarizes the unit characteristic data by occupation, including the size of the sample, the average unit size in the sample, and the mean first term/career ratio of the sample. Although a number of factors contribute to the typical experience mix for work units within a given occupation—such as the nature of the work, the degree of technical difficulty associated with the work, the fineness of classification of the occupational specialty, etc.—the sample does conform to our expectations in general with respect to the criterion of technical difficulty and first term/career ratios, namely that more difficult occupations are associated with lower first term/career ratios.

Table 6

FIRST TERM/CAREER RATIOS (CRYPTOGRAPHIC REPAIR SPECIALITY)

```
MISC / DSPLAY                                   306X0

    VBL:        2 Total              Mean Unit Size = 43.6
    MIN:            0.0      Mean first term/career
    MAX:           93.00                 ratio = 1.42/1

         1.    0
         2.    0
         3.    2
         4.    2
         5.    4
         6.   21 **
         7.   24 **
         8.   26 **
         9.   55 *****
        10.   81 ********
        11.   53 *****
        12.   22 **
        13.   16 *
        14.   38 ***
       ─────────────────────────────────────────────────
        15.   73 *******
        16.   99 *********
        17.   38 ***
        18.   25 **
        19.   34 ***
        20.    0
        21.   84 ********
        22.    6
        23.   31 ***
        24.   44 ****
        25.    1
        26.   33 ***
        27.   34 ***
        28.   18 *
        29.   39 ***
        30.   10 *
        31.   17 *
        32.   45 ****
        33.    0
        34.   27 **
        35.   11 *
        36.    0
        37.    0
        38.   21 **
        39.   12 *
        40.    0
        41.   21 **
        42.    0
        43.    1
        44.   11 *
        45.    0
        46.    0
        47.    0
        48.    0
        49.    0
        50.    0
        51.    6
```

Table 7

FIRST TERM/CAREER RATIOS (AEROSPACE GROUND EQUIPMENT REPAIR SPECIALITY)

```
MISC / DSPLAY                              421X3

    VBL:        2 Total        Mean Unit Size  = 19.8
    MIN:              0.0      Mean first term
    MAX:            217.00          ratio  = 2.30/1

            1.    0
            2.    0
            3.    0
            4.    1
            5.    4
            6.   15 *
            7.   11 *
            8.   19 *
            9.   32 ***
           10.   36 ***
           11.   39 ***
           12.   16 *
           13.   23 **
           14.   29 **
           15.   53 *****
           16.   99 *********
           17.   52 *****
           18.   58 *****
           19.   31 ***
           20.   25 **
           21.   68 ******
           22.   52 *****
           23.   47 ****
           24.   67 ******
           25.   52 *****
           26.   57 *****
           27.   21 **
           28.   24 **
           29.   23 **
           30.   13 *
           31.   17 *
           32.   20 **
           33.   26 **
           34.   17 *
           35.    9
           36.    0
           37.    0
           38.    9
           39.   10 *
           40.    4
           41.   13 *
           42.    0
           43.    1
           44.    8
           45.    0
           46.    0
           47.    3
           48.    0
           49.    2
           50.    0
           51.    3
```

Table 8

UNIT CHARACTERISTIC DATA BY OCCUPATION

AFSC	Description	Sample Size	Mean Unit Size	Mean First Term/ Career Ratio Per Unit
304X4	Ground Radio Repairman	653	40.3	2.23
306X0	Electronic Communications Equipment Repairman	386	43.6	1.42
326X0	Avionics Aerospace Ground Equipment Specialist	93	27.2	1.92
326X1	Integrated Avionic Component Specialist	145	138.8	1.83
326X2	Integrated Avionic Systems Specialist	216	195.8	2.34
421X3	Aerospace Ground Equipment Repairman	462	64.6	1.92
422X1	Aircraft Environmental Systems Repairman	185	19.8	2.30
431X1	Aircraft Maintenance Specialist	570	341.9	1.40
542X0	Electrician	143	15.7	2.00
543X0	Electrical Power Production Specialist	271	22.1	2.61
571X0	Fire Protection Specialist	178	50.6	2.78
622X0	Cook	121	36.6	2.27
631X0	Fuels Specialist	349	82.0	2.76
647X0	Materials Facility Specialist	182	64.0	1.59
671X3	Accounting Specialist	122	32.7	6.08
902X0	Hospital Corpsman	346	122.5	4.76
981X0	Dental Specialist	170	57.0	5.68

Total Sample 4592

V. DATA ANALYSIS

Our objective in analyzing the productivity measures contained in the Enlisted Utilization Survey data base is to specify the parameters of the labor aggregation functions described in Section I. Auxiliary to this fundamental issue are questions concerning the proper specification of the aggregation function in general, the nature of the estimated productivity relationships with respect to actual substitution potentials, and, finally, questions regarding the quality of the data set and the reliability of the results.

Specifically, the productivity analysis will consider (1) the potential for substitution between first term and career personnel and (2) substitution between various experience categories of first term personnel. Given the estimates of opportunities for substitution, one can ask whether or not the nested constant elasticity of substitution aggregation function is a good specification of the aggregation function between first term and career labor. Finally, questions relating to the quality of the data set and hence to the reliability of the results will be addressed.

The section includes:

- A review of the basic methodology and the proposed productivity model.
- The specific estimating technique and results of the first term aggregation analysis.
- The estimating technique and results of the aggregated first term/career productivity model.
- The presentation of the resultant parameter estimates of the first term/ career labor aggregation functions.

The need for aggregate measures of the supply of labor services to specific military missions arises when we seek to determine the marginal contribution to military effectiveness of a variety of labor categories and how these contributions are affected by changes in labor quality and quantity. This requirement derives from the basic conditions of economic efficiency in production summarized by

$$\frac{MP_c}{MP_f} = \frac{MC_c}{MC_f} \, . \tag{17}$$

To specify the relationship between the contribution of various labor categories and military effectiveness, we can postulate aggregate production function for any military mission:

$$E = f(K, L_f, L_c) \tag{18}$$

where E =   output (readiness or effectiveness) of a particular military mission,

       K =   all non-labor inputs to the specific mission,

       L_f =   the first term labor inputs to the specific mission,

       L_c =   the career labor inputs to the specific mission.

Assuming that (18) can be legitimately rewritten as

$$E = F\left[K, g(L_f, L_c)\right],\tag{19}$$

the task is then to find proper specification of

$$L^* = g(L_f, L_c),\tag{20}$$

where L^* is the total supply of labor to the specific mission.

The assumption that the aggregation function in (18) is separable in (19) cannot be tested in the current framework owing to lack of data on capital stocks and other non-labor inputs for the military occupations included in the sample. This implies that levels of non-labor inputs have no bearing on the relative marginal productivities of different types of labor inputs. As a result, we have excluded the possibility of differences in the degree of complementarity between non-labor inputs and various types of labor.

The standard economic assumption, all else being the same, does not strictly obtain in this case. Capital stock per worker and the specific composition of output are likely to vary greatly among specific work units in the sample for specific occupations. Furthermore, the data refer not to a single production process but to service-wide aggregates. Thus, estimates of the marginal rate of substitution and elasticity of substitution between first term and career labor are not strictly identified parameters of some underlying technical relationship or production function. They reflect the partial elasticity of substitution between L_f and L_c, the degree of complementarity between each of the two types of labor and the excluded factors of production, and the composition of the specific demand each unit faces. We would, of course, like to estimate a function that would tell us the effect of each of the influences (taken separately) on the marginal productivities of different types of labor, but we simply cannot.

Given these limitations, the estimation problem is one of specifying changes in relative marginal productivity of factors as the composition of the military labor force changes. The economic concept of the elasticity of substitution between first term and career labor is a measure that explicitly reflects this relationship and is defined as

$$\sigma_{f,c} = -\frac{d \log \dfrac{L_f}{L_c}}{d \log \dfrac{MP_f}{MP_c}},\tag{21}$$

hence incorporating the marginal rate of substitution MP_f/MP_c.

We would expect these relationships to differ by occupation. In terms of the experience mix, the overall military labor force composition has not changed substantially over time. Thus the best available estimates are elasticities estimated for specific occupations from a cross section of work units substantially different in experience mix.

The proposed general specification of the labor aggregation function defined in (20) is the constant elasticity of substitution function, where first term and career labor are the sole inputs to the function. However, since experience within a given occupation is a continuous variable, the disaggregation of military labor by first term and career personnel is as much an analytic convenience as it is an accurate reflection of production reality. Thus, conceptually, there are an infinite number of labor categories within an occupation based on experience alone. The question then arises as to the proper form of aggregation of the two key labor types. As previously mentioned, for purposes of this analysis we have adopted a nonweighted linear aggregation of career labor. That is, we have assumed that the value of all career inputs to military production within a specific occupation are equal. Although uncertain, the implications of this assumption are likely to systematically understate the value of career labor and thus to overstate the cost effectiveness of first term inputs. With respect to first term labor, however, the appropriate form of aggregation is extremely important. Since changes in productivity over a first term of service are likely to be substantial and since these differences are compressed in a shorter time frame, inappropriate aggregation methods will likely generate substantial errors in the overall estimation process.[1]

The typical approach to the problem of aggregation of first term labor has been to treat it as a single composite factor with the component first term subgroups being weighted by their respective relative productivities.[2] This treatment implicitly assumes an infinite elasticity of substitution between different categories of first term labor. It is natural to question whether or not this is, in fact, the relevant case and to hypothesize that the more general constant elasticity of substitution function might be a more realistic aggregation of first term labor. Thus, we have proposed a nested or tiered constant elasticity of substitution model as the labor aggregation function, where the labor index of specialty output is a CES function in first term and career labor, and the first term input to a model is itself a CES function in specific first term experience categories. The general form of the productivity model to be estimated for each Air Force occupation included in the assembled data base is of the form

$$E_i = \left[a_1 \, L^*_{fi}{}^{-\rho_i} + a_2 \, L_{ci}{}^{-\rho_i} \right]^{-\frac{1}{\rho_i}}, \tag{22}$$

$$L^*_{fi} = \left[\sum_{i=1}^{n} a_i \, L_{fji}{}^{-\theta_i} \right]^{-\frac{1}{\theta_i}}, \tag{23}$$

where

$$\sum_{i=1}^{n} a_i = a_1 + a_2 = 1 ,$$

---

[1] For additional evidence of this effect see sample productivity profiles presented in Albrecht and Gay (1977).

[2] This is the case in each of the previous attempts to analytically address the first term/career issue; Smith (1964); Fisher (1970).

$$-1 < \rho_i = \frac{1 - \sigma_1}{\sigma_1} < \infty, \qquad i = 1, \ldots, n,$$

$$-1 < \theta_i = \frac{1 - \sigma_j}{\sigma_j} < \infty.$$

ESTIMATING TECHNIQUE AND ANALYTIC RESULTS: FIRST TERM AGGREGATION

The basic analytic problems associated with the aggregation of labor types within a first term of service are those of categorization and estimation. *Categorization* refers to the problem of determining feasible and reasonable sets of experience categories within a first term. If the classifications are too coarse, there is a risk that a single category might encompass several heterogeneous groups and as a result would not have strongly identifiable properties of its own. On the other hand, the finer the classification, the more difficult it would be to find plausible groupings of categories with the first term, and the greater would be the problems with deficiences in the data. *Estimation* concerns the problem of determining elasticities of substitution between various first term experience categories, both to guide in the development of appropriate experience categories and to provide parameter estimates for the first tier of the nested CES function once specific first experience categories have been determined.

It would be ideal to categorize first term personnel as finely as possible with respect to on-the-job experience and then to use elasticity estimates as a guide for the formulation of consistent aggregated categories. One technique that would satisfy these ideal conditions would be to derive estimates of the pairwise elasticity of substitution between different pairs of experience categories within a first term and then to use the associated t-statistics of these estimates as the aggregation rule.[3] Specifically, an equation of the form

$$\log (MP_i/MP_j)_k = a + b_{ij} \log (L_i/L_j)_k + u_k, \, k = 1, \ldots, n, \qquad (24)$$

where k subscripts refer to specific work unit observations, could be used to estimate the elasticities of substitution between pairs of first term experience categories. Naturally, it is assumed that the true b_{ij} is constant within each specific kth work unit. Since the elasticity of substitution equals

$$\sigma_{ij} = - \frac{d \log L_i/L_j)}{d \log (MP_i/MP_j)} = - \frac{1}{b_{ij}}, \qquad (25)$$

t-ratios computed for the estimates of b_{ij} would provide a means for determining homogeneous categories of first term labor. This follows from the null hypothesis of the t-test, namely that the true value of b_{ij} is zero. Since this hypothesis is

---

[3] See Bowles (1970) and Dougherty (1971) for a detailed discussion of the ideal method.

equivalent to a hypothesis that the elasticity of substitution is infinite, cases where the estimated value of b_{ij} cannot be statistically distinguished from zero can be combined by linear aggregation and treated as part of a single homogeneous category.[4]

For purposes of this analysis, however, feasibility constraints precluded utilization of this technique. The problems associated with implementing the ideal pairwise estimating technique derive both from the size of the data set and from estimation problems associated with the required reorientation of the data set from a trainee-based data set to a unit-based data set.

From (24) we find that the unit of observation for the pairwise estimating procedure is the specific work unit, subscript k. Thus, the data required for each observation in an analysis of any ij first term pair would be an estimate of the marginal rate of substitution between the two pairs in each unit and the actual input ratio of the two catgories in each work unit. Disaggregation of first term inputs by month of service would at least entail one productivity estimate and one member of the unit serving in each of 48 different experience categories. Since, however, from Table 8, it can be seen that many occupations in the sample have an average unit size less than 48, this level of disaggregation would be infeasible. Furthermore, since the data set rarely includes more than 10 or 12 specific productivity ratings per work unit, the choices among experience categories within a unit would be limited and in many cases would be inconsistent across units. The specific composition of the data set limits our ability to disaggregate first term inputs much beyond rather coarse groupings. More important, however, are the estimation problems associated with constructing the relevant variables required for estimating the pairwise elasticities from variables extant on the data set.

It will be recalled that the basic data for each observation is the productivity rating for a specific trainee; all other data such as unit composition variables are auxiliary to that unit of observation. But as we have just argued, the relevant data points for the estimation of pairwise elasticities are specific work units. The translation of trainee-based observations to unit-based observations in the case of intra-first term experience analysis is an extremely cumbersome task.[5]

Even the simplest form of aggregation, however, would present an enormous

[4] This, of course, is not strictly the case since the hypothesis that the true value of b_{ij} is equal to zero is consistent with *both* the hypothesis that the elasticity is infinite and that the elasticity is *zero*. These latter two hypotheses cannot, therefore, be discriminated from each other on the basis of a statistical analysis of b_{ij} alone. However, one may infer the correct hypothesis by a simple analysis of the data. A graphical analysis of the relationship between the two categories of interest and their estimated marginal rates of substitution will indicate by its shape the relevant hypothesis. The more the resultant graph approaches a right angle, the more likely the fixed factor case obtains, and vice versa. The results of many such graphs for the EUS data set indicate that the infinite hypothesis is the correct hypothesis; hence we refer to the T-test on b_{ij} as equivalent to a test of the infinite elasticity hypothesis. I am indebted to D. Chu of The Rand Corporation for suggesting this method of verification to me.

[5] For example, let us take the case of the pairwise comparison between the ith and jth first term experience categories. To transform the data from trainee- to unit-based observations, two variables must be constructed. One variable would consist of the actual input ratio of the ith to jth categories within each unit. Since the unit composition data on the assembled data base consist of a vector of specific counts of several experience categories within the unit, the input ratio variable could be relatively easily constructed by aggregating the counts over the relevant subcategories and taking the ratio of the aggregated counts of the ith and jth groups. However, with respect to the marginal rate of substitution variable, the computation procedure would be much more complex. In this case, trainees sampled from the same work unit would need to be identified. Once identified, each trainee would have to be categorized into either the ith or jth experience group. Relative productivity estimates of each experience group would then have to be aggregated from each of the individual productivity estimates to provide an estimate of the group's composite productivity.

computational problem given the large number of trainees per occupation and units included in the sample. Iterating this procedure to find the best categorization of different first term inputs even among very coarse groupings would clearly be prohibitive in terms of time and cost. The ideal sort of approach to the problems of categorization and estimation is unobtainable because of data set limitations and data management problems in transforming the data set from trainee-based to unit-based observations.

To deal with the categorization problem, an alternative method to identify appropriate categories of first term labor was adopted. This method was sufficiently broad to be supported by the data, yet provided some basis for confidence in the homogeneity of the categories a priori. Specifically, regression analyses were conducted for each occupation to identify the categories of first term experience that account for the greatest amount of variation in first term productivity estimates. The procedure involved regressing a series of indicator variables, corresponding to various classifications of first term job experience, on the productivity estimates.

Although we would expect that these regressions would yield different results and hence different indications of appropriate categorizations for each occupation, three points in a first term seemed to provide natural breaks over all the observed occupations: around six months, around one year, and around one year and a half. However, the specific breakpoints in each occupation varied about the six month, one year, and eighteen month point, and since analytically it is desirable to be parsimonious with respect to the number of different models estimated, three specific categorizations were selected which seemed to best reflect the productivity data: 0-8 and 9-(48-N) months of experience where N represents the numbers of months of training; 0-11 and 12-(48-N) months of experience; and 0-14 and 15-(48-N) months of experience. As one would expect, the experience classification for each occupation is related to the relative technical skill of each occupation. That is, more technically demanding occupations are associated with a categorization that tends to break first term labor at more advanced experience levels; conversely, lower skill occupations are associated with categorizations that reflect distinctions of first term labor much earlier in the first term of service. That these categorizations are reasonable ones for each occupation is borne out in the conduct of the actual elasticity analysis.

For the estimation problem, the alternative approach adopted retains the flexibility and precision of the ideal method but does not impose the substantial data management problems in orienting the data set for the analysis. This approach involves a two-stage estimation of the parameters in Eq. (24), utilizing a technique deriving from the literature of the omitted variable case and demonstrated by Griliches (1957).

To deal with the computational problems posed by the estimation technique of pairwise elasticities of substitution between various first term experience categories reflected in Eq. (24), we have adopted an approach that allows for estimation of the parameters in Eq. (24) in a two-stage process. This approach retains the desirable characteristics of the general formulation, but avoids the substantial data management problems associated with the one-stage procedure. And, it will be shown, the expected value of the estimates of b_{ij} and, hence σ_{ij}, are identical in both cases.

Specifically, by taking logs of both sides and rearranging terms, we can rewrite Eq. (24) as

$$\ln \text{MP}_i = \frac{a_i}{a_j} + b_1 \ln \frac{L_i}{L_j} + b_2 \ln \text{MP}_j + u. \tag{26}$$

If we then treat MP_j as an omitted variable in Eq. (24) and estimate b_1 by ordinary least squares, we find that the true b_1 is equal to the observed $b_1 + pb_2$, where b_2 is the coefficient of the omitted variable MP_j, and p summarizes the covariation of the excluded and included variables. If we assume that b_2 equals 1 from Eq. (24), then p equals the least square's coefficient of the included variable on the excluded variable, in this case $\ln \text{MP}_j$ on L_i/L_j.

Consider the general multiple regression problem

$$Y = XB + u, \tag{27}$$

where Y is a column vector of values taken by the dependent variable, X is a matrix of values of all independent variables, B is a column vector of parameters we want to estimate, and u is a column vector of disturbances with zero expectation. However, let us say that we do not use X, but $\bar{X}$ in estimating procedure where $\bar{X}$ is a different matrix of independent variables; for example, where $\bar{X}$ is equal to X except that it has one or more columns less than X. Thus, instead of estimating Eq. (27), we estimate

$$Y = \bar{X}B + u. \tag{28}$$

Assume that we estimate $\bar{B}$ by the method of least squares. Then the estimate of $\bar{B}$, b, will be given by

$$b = (\bar{X}'\bar{X})^{-1} \bar{X}'Y. \tag{29}$$

Taking the expectation of b, we get

$$E(b) = E(\bar{X}'\bar{X})^{-1} \bar{X}' (XB+u) = (\bar{X}'\bar{X})^{-1} \bar{X}' XB. \tag{30}$$

Let $(\bar{X}'\bar{X})^{-1} \bar{X}'X = p$, then

$$E(b) = pB. \tag{31}$$

If we look at the formula for p it can be seen that the elements of p are the coefficients in the regression of each column of X on $\bar{X}$; that is, they are the coefficients of the least squares regression of each of the "true" variables X on all of the included variables.

If we exclude variable X_k from the analysis, the expectation of the estimates of the included coefficients is given by

$$E(b_1) = b_i + p_{ik} b_k. \tag{32}$$

In the two-variable case this is simply

$$E(b_1) = b_1 + p_{12} b_2, \tag{33}$$

where b_2 is the coefficient of the omitted variable in (28) (recall we assume this to equal 1 from (24)) and p_{12} from (31) is simply the coefficient from the auxiliary regression of X on $\bar{X}$.

In short, the procedure is to regress $\ln \text{MP}_i$ on L_i/L_j to estimate b_1 and then to regress $\ln \text{MP}_j$ on L_i/L_j to estimate p_{12}. Thus the overall estimate of $b_{ij} = b_1 +$

p_{12}. The advantage of the two-stage approach over the one-stage estimator is that because it requires only one estimate of marginal productivity per observation, the variables required for two-stage estimation already exist on the data files as currently organized. A critical assumption in the equality of the one- and two-stage approaches is that the rows of X and $\bar{X}$ are the same in each case.[6] Although we will discuss the validity of this assumption in the context of the actual estimation results, it is worthwhile to mention at this point that in each of the two-stage estimation cases the rows of X and $\bar{X}$ were virtually identical for each occupation. Thus the expected values of the two b_{ij}'s were the same.

In sum, the estimation procedure adopted for specification of the first tier of the aggregation function given by (23) involves the estimation of the first term elasticity parameter in Eq. (24) through a two-stage process. The categorization of first term aggregate inputs to the model is provided by an auxiliary analysis of the relationship between first term experience and productivity. The variables required for the two-stage estimation of (24) for each occupation included in the sample are estimates of the marginal relative productivity of the ith and jth first term categories and the input ratios of the ith and jth labor types in each operational unit included in the sample. In the following subsection we discuss the creation of these variables and the data set preparation for the estimation procedure, as well as the results of the first tier analysis.

PRODUCTIVITY INPUTS TO THE FIRST TERM MODEL

The preparation of the EUS productivity data set for use as a data base in estimating the parameters in Eq. (24) has two important aspects: the editing of the raw data with respect to validity and reliability checks, and the control for subjective bias in the supervisory estimates.

As previously mentioned, the specific data point used as the productivity variable in this analysis is the supervisor's estimate of an individual's "current" net contribution to unit production.[7] The reasons for this choice are detailed in Section II, but essentially we expected that this estimate would be the most accurate reflection of productivity and thus would minimize reliance on the supervisor's forecasts. Specific observations of current productivity were included in the analysis sample if (1) the supervisor indicated that he was familiar with the specific trainee's work, (2) the supervisor making the rating answered the test question of concept comprehension correctly, (3) the supervisor provided estimates for all time periods for both the specific trainee and the typical trainee (to provide a check on consistency), (4) the supervisor's estimate of the productivity of the typical trainee was less than 100 percent in the first month and greater than zero after four years of service (an additional check on concept comprehension), and (5) the first term/career ratio for the individual's work unit was within two standard deviations of the mean ratio of the occupation (to ensure that errors in data accumulation or that extremely undermanned or overmanned units would not exert undue influence on

---

[6] I am indebted to Professor Robert Solow of MIT for pointing out to me the importance of this assumption for the econometric analysis.

[7] Recall that the data base includes estimates of relative productivity for several points in a first term of service.

the results). Editing criteria so imposed reduced the initial sample size by less than 10 percent overall, and never exceeded 15 percent for any specific occupation.

The productivity estimates in the edited sample were then adjusted to control for subjective bias by a procedure using the supervisor's estimate of the productivity of the typical trainee. Basically, the technique was to adjust individual productivity estimates by subtracting residuals from auxiliary regressions on the supervisor's estimates of the typical trainee's productivity. These regressions served to remove the systematic bias inherent in supervisor's ratings of specific individuals, while maintaining the effects of unit composition in the ratings. Thus, auxiliary regressions of unit input ratios on supervisor's estimates of the typical trainee's productivity would leave the residuals of the regressions composed solely of systematic bias and random error absent the effect of input ratios.

The independent variables for the edited sample were constructed by summing across portions of the experience category vector of variables that refer to each unit's specific labor composition. Thus, for any observation in the sample, the construction of the L_i/L_j input ratio variable simply involved summation across the various experience categories. Thus,

$$L_i = \sum_{i=1}^{N} I_i, \quad L_j = \sum_{i=N+1}^{48} I_i,$$

where I_i = the number of individuals serving a first term with i months of service in each specific work unit,

N = the last month of service category included in the ith category of first term labor for each occupation.

RESULTS OF THE FIRST TERM ANALYSIS

The results of the first term parameter estimation are presented in Table 9, which shows the estimated elasticity of substitution between the categories of first term labor, the computed t-ratio for the aggregated coefficient from which the elasticity is derived, and the categories of first term labor used for the estimation. Recall that the estimate of the elasticity derives from the estimated coefficient in (21) since

$$\sigma_{ij} = \frac{1}{-\beta_{ij}}$$

and that our estimate of $\hat{\beta}_{ij}$ derives from a two-stage procedure where

$$\hat{\beta}_{ij} = \beta_i + \beta_j.$$

Hence

$$\sigma_{ij} = \frac{1}{-(\beta_i + \beta_j)}. \tag{34}$$

Table 9

Estimates of Substitution Elasticities for First Term Aggregation

AFSC	Description	$\hat{\sigma}_{ij}$	t-ratio	L_i, L_j Categories
326X0	Avionics Aerospace Ground Equipment Specialist	2.16	2.49[*]	0 to 14 months service and 15 to 48 months service
326X1	Integrated Avionic Component Specialist	1.11	3.04[*]	0 to 14 months service and 15 to 48 months service
326X2	Integrated Avionic Systems Specialist	2.65	1.98[*]	0 to 14 months service and 15 to 48 months service
304X4	Ground Radio Repairman	9.39	1.75[*]	0 to 14 months service and 15 to 48 months service
306X0	Electronic Communications Equipment Repairman	8.09	2.25[*]	0 to 14 months service and 15 to 48 months service
421X3	Aerospace Ground Equipment Repairman	3.50	4.30[*]	0 to 11 months service and 12 to 48 months service
422X1	Aircraft Environmental Systems Repairman	3.77	2.35[*]	0 to 8 months service and 9 to 48 months service
431X1	Aircraft Maintenance Specialist	3.70	2.48[*]	0 to 8 months service and 9 to 48 months service
542X0	Electrician	0.84	6.70[*]	0 to 8 months service and 9 to 48 months service
543X0	Electrical Power Production Specialist	4.52	1.95[*]	0 to 11 months service and 12 to 48 months service
571X0	Fire Protection Specialist	1.76	3.01[*]	0 to 11 months service and 12 to 48 months service
622X0	Cook	4.76	2.12[*]	0 to 8 months service and 9 to 48 months service
631X0	Fuels Specialist	1.94	2.57[*]	0 to 8 months service and 9 to 48 months service
647X0	Materials Facility Specialist	1.10	4.30[*]	0 to 11 months service and 12 to 48 months service
671X3	Accounting Specialist	2.55	1.87	0 to 8 months service and 9 to 48 months service
902X0	Hospital Corpsman	4.40	2.45[*]	0 to 8 months service and 9 to 48 months service
981X1	Dental Specialist	7.04	2.19[*]	0 to 8 months service and 9 to 48 months service

[*]Significant at the .01 confidence level.

The most important result reflected in Table 9 is that on the basis of the regression analysis, we can reject the hypothesis that the elasticity of substitution between different categories of first term labor is infinite, and hence the hypothesis that the linear method of aggregation is in all cases the best method of aggregation.

In all but two of the occupational cases analyzed, this result is confirmed with statistical confidence. However, even though in several cases a significantly non-infinite elasticity is estimated, the estimate itself is sufficiently high to be reasonably well reflected by a linear aggregation method over a reasonable range of actual substitutions (say, cases where the elasticity exceeds 5.0). The pattern of estimated elasticities, however, provides no strong indication of the relationship between technical difficulty by occupation and the elasticity of substitution between groups within a first term of service, as we might have expected a priori. But many intervening factors might tend to obscure this relationship within a first term—for example, the accuracy of the categories predetermined for the analysis, the distribution of mental categories within each occupation, the effectiveness of formal training, etc.—all of which would contribute to our inability to observe a strongly identifiable relationship that we may have anticipated a priori.

An additional inference can be derived from Table 9 regarding the credibility of the productivity data set from which the estimates were derived. Specifically, the fact that the estimates of the elasticity of substitution were both right-signed and significant in all but two cases indicates that the underlying productivity data set is of high quality. The relationship between specific productivity estimates and actual input composition of each work unit is extremely subtle, and one would not expect to see it significantly reflected in an analysis of supervisory ratings where this particular use of the data was not initially intended. The fact that the supervisors' ratings of specific individuals' productivity were significantly related to unit characteristics—although made with no knowledge that these estimates could or would be related to the specific labor composition of the unit from which they were drawn—lends credibility to the productivity estimates.

In terms of the specification of the first term model given by (23), the estimates of the elasticity of substitution reflected in Table 9 can be transformed into values of θ_{ij}, the substitution parameter in (23), by the relationship:

$$-\beta_{ij} = \frac{1}{1 + \theta_{ij}} = \frac{1}{\sigma_{ij}} . \tag{35}$$

The distribution parameters in (23), the a_i, and hence the $a_j = (1 - a_i)$, can be determined directly from the data and the estimated parameter of substitution given the general formulation of the parameter from the definition of the CES function. Thus

$$\frac{a_i}{a_j} = \frac{\overline{MP}_i}{\overline{MP}_j} \frac{L_i}{L_j} \left(\frac{L_i}{L_j}\right)^{\theta_{ij} - 1} \tag{36}$$

and

$$a_j = 1 - a_i,$$

where $\overline{MP}_i =$ the mean marginal productivity of the ith
category,

$\overline{MP}_j =$ the mean marginal productivity of the jth
category,

$\theta_{ij} =$ the estimated substitution parameter from the
two-stage estimation of (24).

Table 10 presents the first tier specifications of the aggregation model given by (22) for each of the occupations included in the sample where the model is of the form:

$$L^*_f = \left[a_i \, L_{f_i}^{-\theta_{ij}} + a_j \, L_{f_j}^{-\theta_{ij}} \right]^{\frac{1}{-\theta_{ij}}} . \tag{23}$$

An additional element of Table 10 consists of the parameter estimates of an alternative formulation of the first term aggregation model, the weighted linear aggregation model in which case the parameters γ_i and γ_j represent the weights of the two categories of first term labor predetermined for each occupation in the sample. The general form of the model is

$$\gamma_i \, L_i + \gamma_j \, L_j = L^*_f. \tag{37}$$

Implicit in this formulation is the assumption that the elasticity of substitution between the first term subcategories is infinite. The weights γ_i and γ_j reflect the mean marginal productivity of the two groups. Since these two parameters reflect marginal relative productivities rather than factor proportions, they need not sum to one. We include this alternative formulation of the first tier model because it will provide an additional check on the validity of the hypothesis that elasticities of substitution are infinite and because several of the estimated elasticities, although significantly different from infinity, are sufficiently large to be approximated by the linear aggregation model. We expect that this alternative formulation of L^*_f as an input to the general model given by (22) should provide similar results to those of the CES formulation in most cases; however, these results may not be as statistically significant as the CES inputs because the first tier analysis results indicate that linearly aggregated measures provide a statistically inferior model of production reality.

For each observation in the data set, two values of L^*_f were computed for each work unit—one from the estimated CES first term model and the other from the weighted linear aggregation model. These values can be used as inputs to the first term/career CES model given by

$$L^*_i = \left[a^*_{1_i} \, L^{*-\rho_i}_{f_i} + a_{2_i} \, L_{c_i}^{-\rho_i} \right]^{-\frac{1}{\rho_i}} , \tag{38}$$

Table 10

SPECIFICATIONS OF FIRST TERM AGGREGATION FUNCTION:
CES AND LINEAR MODELS

AFSC	α_i	α_j	$-\theta_{ij}$	$-\dfrac{1}{\theta_{ij}}$	γ_i	γ_j
326X0	.494	.505	.539	1.85	.300	.710
326X1	.490	.510	.099	10.1	.160	.449
326X2	.805	.195	.624	1.60	.275	.616
304X4	.318	.681	.894	1.11	.327	.578
306X0	.363	.636	.876	1.14	.038	.546
421X3	.301	.699	.716	1.39	.215	.465
422X1	.030	.970	.735	1.35	.073	.502
423X0	.607	.392	.880	1.13	.030	.417
431X1	.025	.975	.735	1.35	.036	.568
542X0	.070	.930	-.190	-5.25	.082	.441
543X0	.115	.884	.780	1.28	.142	.417
571X0	.125	.875	.435	2.20	.121	.508
622X0	.018	.981	.797	1.27	.032	.562
631X0	.040	.956	.487	2.05	.307	.457
647X0	.490	.510	.099	9.90	.167	.589
671X3	.140	.860	.609	1.64	.056	.645
902X0	.350	.650	.772	1.29	.049	.658
981X1	.056	.944	.858	1.16	.104	.766

where $L^*_i =$ total labor services available to the ith military mission,

$L^*_{f_i} =$ an index of the total first term labor inputs to the ith military mission,

$L_{ci} =$ total career labor input to the ith military mission,

and

where $\rho_i =$ the substitution parameter of the CES function between a first term labor index and career labor in the ith mission,

$a^*_{1_i}, a_{2_i} =$ the distribution parameters of the CES function for a first term labor index and career labor in the ith mission.

ESTIMATING TECHNIQUE AND ANALYTIC RESULTS:
FIRST TERM/CAREER AGGREGATION

Given the estimation of two aggregation models for first term labor inputs to specific military missions, the problem remains as to the specification of the first term/career aggregation function given above. The substitution parameter in (38) can be estimated via Eq. (24). Thus,

$$\ln\left(\frac{MP^*_f}{MP_c}\right) = \alpha + b_{1,2}\,\ln\left(\frac{L^*_f}{L_c}\right) + u \tag{39}$$

will provide an estimate of the elasticity of substitution between the first term aggregate and career labor, as well as an estimate of the substitution parameter in Eq. (38), since again

$$-\beta_{1,2} = \frac{1}{1+\rho_{1,2}} = \frac{1}{\sigma_{1,2}}. \tag{40}$$

Since the productivity data in the EUS are already in the form of productivity relative to a journeyman specialist in each specific work unit from which the observation is drawn, there is no need for aggregation within specific units; hence (38) may be estimated directly, without recourse to the two-stage method adopted in the estimation of the first term aggregate. However, although the results of the first term aggregation model provide a value of the first term index, L^*_f of each unit, the actual productivity measures do not correspond to measures of the first term index relative to career personnel. Each observation in the EUS data set corresponds to an estimate of the marginal productivity of the ith first term labor category relative to a fully qualified specialist. Thus, instead of

$$\frac{\dfrac{\partial L^*}{\partial L^*_f}}{\dfrac{\partial L^*}{\partial L_c}} = \frac{MP^*_f}{MP_c} \tag{41}$$

we have

$$\frac{\dfrac{\partial L^*}{\partial L_{fi}}}{\dfrac{\partial L^*}{\partial L_c}} = \frac{MP_{fi}}{MP_c} \tag{42}$$

where L^* = total labor available to the ith mission. Hence the data from the EUS cannot be used to estimate the independent variable directly. However, expanding (22) to include the specification of L^*_f given by (23) and taking the partial derivative in the expanded form of L^* with respect to any L_{fi} we find that

$$\frac{\dfrac{\partial L^{*}}{\partial L_{fi}}}{\dfrac{\partial L^{*}}{\partial L_{c}}} = \left[\frac{a_1}{a_2}\left(\frac{L_f^{*}}{L_c}\right)^{-\rho-1}\right]\frac{L_f^{*}\left[a_i\,L_{fi}^{\;-\theta_{ij}}\right]}{\left[a_i\,L_{fi}^{\;-\theta_{ij}} + a_j\,L_{ij}^{\;-\theta_{ij}}\right]L_{fi}} \tag{43}$$

and multiplying both sides by

$$\frac{\left[a_i\,L_{fi}^{\;-\theta_{ij}} + a_j L_j^{\;-\theta_{ij}}\right]L_{fi}}{L_f^{*}\left[a_i\,(L_{fi})^{-\theta_{ij}}\right]}\;, \tag{44}$$

we find that adjusting the raw data, $\mathrm{MP}_{fi}/\mathrm{MP}_{c}$, by (44), all of whose elements are known from the first term aggregation model, we can use the estimation function given by (39) to find the elasticity of substitution between the first term aggregate and career labor for any given occupation. Hence the expected value of the resultant estimate of $\beta_{1,2}$ will be equal to the expected value of $\beta_{1,2}$ from (39).

Thus, to each observation in the data set a variable corresponding to the value of (44) was computed and appended using the values of a_i, a_j θ_{ij}, and L_f^{*} from the appropriate first term aggregation model and the unit data from which the observation was drawn.

Table 11 summarizes the results of the first term/career estimating procedure for two different models of first term labor aggregation—the CES aggregation model and the weighted linear or infinite elasticity model.

The estimated elasticities of substitution between the first term index and career labor are given, as well as the t-ratios corresponding to a test of the hypothesis that the estimated elasticity of substitution is significantly different from infinity ($\beta = 0$). Within the first grouping an additional t-ratio is reported which provides a statistical test of the hypothesis that the estimated elasticity of substitution is significantly different from one, that is the implicit assumption in the commonly used Cobb-Douglas function ($\beta = -1$).[8]

A significant relationship between marginal rates of substitution and actual input ratios between first term and career personnel appears to exist, and it is an inverse relationship as expected. That is to say, all other things being equal, the relative marginal productivity of first term to career personnel declines as the ratio of first term to career personnel increases. This result not only supports the particular form of the functional relationship selected for the analysis, but also lends a great deal of credibility to the productivity data set. As we have previously argued, this particular relationship is an extremely subtle one which a data set of low quality would be unlikely to indicate, especially so consistently over a large number of occupational observations.

Within the context of the first set of elasticities, those derived from the CES first term aggregation function, we find that in the vast majority of the cases the estimated elasticity of substitution is significantly different from infinity. This indicates that the commonly adopted assumption of an infinite elasticity of substitution may be inappropriate in most cases. The overall mean of estimated elasticities for the

---

[8] See Fisher (1970); Jacquette and Nelson (1974).

Table 11

ESTIMATES OF SUBSTITUTION ELASTICITIES FOR FIRST
TERM/CAREER FROM CES AND WEIGHTED LINEAR MODELS

AFSC	I (CES)			II (Weighted Linear)		First Term to Career Marginal Rates of Substitution at Current Input Levels
	$\sigma_{1,2}$ (1)	t-ratio $\beta = 0$ (2)	t-ratio $\beta = -1$ (3)	$\sigma_{1,2}$ (4)	t-ratio $\beta = 0$ (5)	
326X0	2.30	1.76	2.28	2.81	0.80	2.20
326X1	1.50	1.96	0.98	1.42	1.80	2.17
326X2	1.25	5.80	1.45	1.58	1.96	2.25
304X4	5.01	2.25	9.09	6.04	1.58	2.15
306X0	5.05	1.78	4.05	5.77	1.09	2.15
421X3	2.57	2.44	3.83	3.05	1.76	1.91
422X1	1.81	4.77	3.86	2.08	1.56	1.95
431X1	2.14	1.88	2.14	1.72	2.46	1.72
542X0	0.82	3.19	0.58	1.42	2.17	1.92
543X0	4.00	1.86	5.58	6.01	0.89	1.92
571X0	4.48	1.69	5.88	5.11	1.26	1.92
622X0	4.00	0.94	2.81	2.23	1.78	1.68
631X0	8.92	0.73	5.78	7.19	.786	1.42
647X0	3.61	8.36	21.9	4.25	1.78	1.35
671X3	4.08	1.85	5.70	5.60	1.12	1.48
902X0	1.71	4.79	3.40	3.01	0.79	1.41
981X1	5.23	1.69	7.15	9.44	1.44	1.45

entire sample of occupations was 3.6, which indicates that in general, while the potential for substitution between first term and career labor exists, this substitution is limited.

Figure 2 illustrates the relationship between the estimated elasticities of substitution between first term and career personnel and occupational skill level as reflected by length of formal training. As anticipated, this relationship is negative: longer training times tend to be associated with lower elasticities of substitution. It can be expected that more technically demanding occupations have more rigid experience requirements and hence have lower elasticities of substitution. Note that two of the most skilled (as indicated by length of formal training) occupations in the sample have very high estimated elasticities of substitution. When formal training becomes very lengthy, say over six months, graduates may be so well prepared that even though their relative productivity in terms of speed and efficiency may be far below more experienced technicians, their substitutability may in fact increase. Thus, while new graduates may be substantially less productive than their senior counterparts, their training may be broad enough that they can, given time, accomplish any job-related task in the work center; hence the elasticity of substitution will be higher. The relationship between marginal rates of substitution and occupational skill level is likewise quite strong,

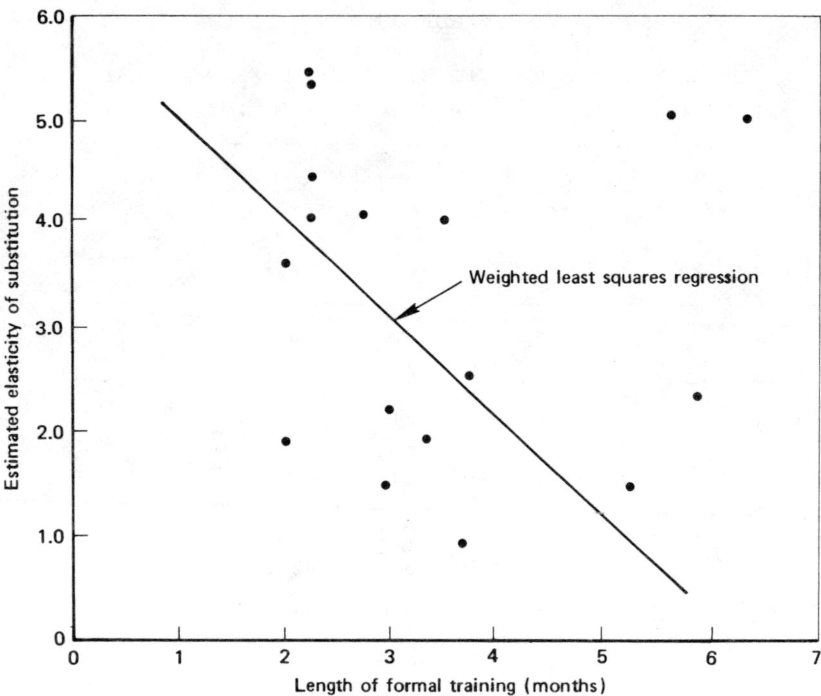

Fig. 2—Relationship between estimated elasticities
of substitution and training time

indicating that for more technically demanding occupations more first term personnel are required to offset the loss of one career laborer.

Taken together the results indicate that the more technically demanding the occupation, the more limited are the substitution opportunities of first term personnel for career personnel, both in terms of the number of first term personnel required to offset career losses and in terms of actual substitutions required to induce changes in the substitution potential at any given point.

An additional hypothesis tested in the context of the nested CES version of the labor aggregation function was that the estimated elasticity of substitution was not significantly different from one, the assumption implicit in the commonly used Cobb Douglas function. The results of this test are reflected by t-ratios in column (3) of Table 11. These findings indicate that in fact the bulk of the cases *can* be significantly discriminated from the unitary elasticity case, by having an estimated elasticity greater than one.

On the basis of these results, we conclude that the adoption of the Cobb-Douglas formulation of the aggregation function would tend to systematically understate the elasticity of substitution between first term and career labor. Taken together with the test of the infinite elasticity case, we find that the two most commonly used aggregation functions—the weighted linear and the Cobb-Douglas—tend to either systematically overstate or understate the elasticity of substitution between first term and career labor. Thus the more general constant elasticity of substitution formulation is superior.

As an additional check on the results from the first term aggregation technique, elasticities of substitution between first term aggregates and career labor were also estimated from the weighted linear aggregation method and are reported in column (4) of Table 11, with the t-ratios associated with the test of infinite elasticity reported in column (5). As anticipated, the results in terms of estimated elasticities are almost identical (the partial correlation coefficient between the two estimated is .8595). The estimates from the infinite elasticity first term aggregation model are slightly higher than those derived from the CES formulation. (The mean for the first group is 3.6, and the mean for the second group is 4.4; however, this is not a statistically significant difference.) Since the infinite elasticity first term model is a statistically inferior reflection of the actual elasticity, the estimates of L^*_1 derived from this model include more unexplained variation and hence tend to drive the resultant first term/career coefficient to zero and the elasticity to infinity. The results of the two versions of the first term/career model show that the CES formulation of first term labor aggregation was more statistically significant than the infinite elasticity aggregation model.

Table 12 arrays the final parameter estimates of the first term/career labor aggregation function of the general form:

$$\left(a^*_1 \ L^{*-\rho}_f + a_2 \ L^{-\rho}_c \right)^{-\frac{1}{\rho}}.$$

Table 12

ESTIMATES OF FIRST TERM/CAREER LABOR AGGREGATION

AFSC	Description	α^*_1	α_2	$-\rho$	$\dfrac{1}{-\rho}$
326X0	Avionics Aerospace Ground Equipment Specialist	.350	.650	.565	1.77
326X1	Integrated Avionic Component Specialist	.368	.631	.333	3.00
326X2	Integrated Avionic Systems Specialist	.325	.675	.200	5.00
304X4	Ground Radio Repairman	.337	.663	.800	1.25
306X0	Electronic Communications Equipment Repairman	.373	.627	.802	1.24
421X3	Aerospace Ground Equipment Repairman	.395	.605	.610	1.63
422X1	Aircraft Environmental Systems Repairman	.386	.613	.447	2.23
431X1	Aircraft Maintenance Specialist	.370	.630	.532	1.87
542X0	Electrician	.376	.624	-.221	-4.52
543X0	Electrical Power Production Specialist	.400	.600	.750	1.33
571X0	Fire Protection Specialist	.370	.630	.777	1.29
622X0	Cook	.405	.595	.750	1.33
631X0	Fuels Specialist	.486	.514	.888	1.12
647X0	Materials Facility Specialist	.431	.569	.723	1.38
671X0	Accounting Specialist	.424	.576	.755	1.32
902X0	Hospital Corpsman	.400	.600	.415	2.41
981X0	Dental Specialist	.404	.506	.809	1.24

Again, the estimates of the elasticity of substitution reflected in Table 11 can be converted to parameter estimates by Eq. (35):

$$\beta = \frac{1}{1 + \rho} = \frac{1}{\sigma} \ .$$

Similarly, the distribution parameters (a^*_1, a_2) can be determined directly from the regression estimates by Eq. (36):

$$\frac{a^*_1}{a_2} = \frac{MP^*_f}{MP_c} \ \frac{L^*_f}{L_c} \left(\frac{L^*_f}{L_c} \right)^{\rho - 1} \ .$$

SUMMARY

We can conclude from the productivity analysis findings that

1. Substitution between first term and career personnel in the production context is feasible, but this substitution cannot be achieved at constant rates indefinitely.
2. Within a first term of service, substitution between various experience categories is also feasible, but as with the former case, this substitution potential is limited.

Both of these conclusions are in direct contradiction to the two most commonly held assumptions regarding the military production process, namely, that military production can only be achieved with fixed proportions of enlisted personnel *or* that a single marginal rate of substitution observed at one particular production point can be applied over all possible production combinations. The findings indicate that, at least for the Air Force occupations in this sample, these latter two hypotheses can be rejected with statistical confidence.

3. Estimated marginal rates of substitution and elasticities of substitution are related to occupational skill level.

Specifically, we find that higher skill level occupations tend to be associated with higher estimates of marginal rates of substitutions and lower elasticities of substitution. Intuitively this result seems reasonable since we would expect that more technically demanding occupations would be associated with longer intervals for new specialists to become qualified, and hence with higher rates of marginal substitution, and that since the level of competence required at the fully qualified level is higher in more technical occupations, the elasticity of substitution would be smaller reflecting the rigidity of the qualified skill requirement.

In sum, these findings support the general conclusion that the Enlisted Utilization Survey data base is credible and thus provides a solid basis for the conduct of productivity analysis like that presented here. Finally, we conclude that the constant elasticity of substitution formulation of the aggregation function in both the first term career and intra-first term cases is superior to either the infinite elasticity or the Cobb-Douglas constant-at-unity elasticity formulation.

VI. FRAMEWORK FOR DECISIONMAKING

How can the findings of the productivity analysis described in Section V be used in minimizing total manpower costs subject to the production constraint introduced in Section II?

The labor aggregation models we have estimated for each occupation can be used to determine marginal rates of substitution—and hence relative marginal products—of first term and career labor at specific production points over a wide range of production alternatives. But we need to measure the relative costs of these two inputs at various levels of utilization in order to determine the least costly combinations of labor at specified effectiveness levels, given the specific form of the resultant cost and productivity functions.

The ideal method one would use to find an optimal mix of first term and career personnel for any occupation would be to minimize the present value of annual total force costs in transition and in the resultant steady state subject to a constant production constraint. The problem could thus be represented by minimizing the value of

$$\sum_{i=0}^{30} (1 + r)^{-i} \left[\sum_{j=1}^{30} W_{ij}L_j \right] + \left[(1 + r)^{-30} \frac{C}{r} \right] = \text{total cost}$$

subject to the constraint,

$$\lambda \left[\left[a_1^* L_f^{*-\rho} + a_2 L_c^{-\rho} \right]^{-\frac{1}{\rho}} - Q_i \right] = 0 ,$$

where

$$L_f = f(w_f) \text{ and } L_c = g(w_c, L_f).$$

Total costs are represented in this system by both the present value of total force transition costs from the initial time interval to the time when the steady state is achieved and by the present value of total force costs in the steady state. Production is held constant in each of the time periods, both during transition and in a steady state, and supply is controlled through supply functions for first term and career labor. The solution to the system would require two stages. First the optimal steady state force structure deriving from a static optimization model would be determined and then the optimal transition phase force structure deriving from some dynamic adjustment model.[1] But our purpose is to gain insight into the production portion of the optimal force structure problem, not to solve the extremely difficult and complex problem of total force structure optimization in transition and

---

[1] The basic methodology for determining optimal force structures in both the static and dynamic framework is described in Munch (1977).

in a steady state. Thus the ideal methodology far exceeds the scope of the current analysis. Other analysts may use our findings to pursue the true optimization problem, but that is not our intent here.

The approach we have adopted is to minimize the total cost of a given force subject to a production constraint in the context of two simple illustrative models, each of which incorporates different assumptions regarding the costs of enlisted labor and its supply. The first model is a simple steady state model where first term and career wages are taken as given by the current wage rates and where it is assumed that sufficient quantities of first term and career labor are available at those wage rates to meet any demand.[2]

The second model explicitly integrates reenlistment supply considerations into the determination of cost. In this case, career wage is a variable as are the two categories of labor and, thus, efficient solutions will include not only specific mixes of first term and career personnel but also an optimal wage required to induce the retention of cost effective additional career personnel.

The advantage of this approach is that it allows for the determination of unbiased cost effective mixes of first term and career labor consistent with the particular conditions of each occupation. For example, in those cases where the current mix or a more junior mix is implied as the cost effective one, the simple steady state model ensures that the solution is unbiased inasmuch as career labor will be systematically underpriced. But in cases where more career personnel are indicated, the supply constrained model ensures that the solution will be unbiased, since the assumptions regarding reenlistment supply are conservative with respect to cost of supply. The specific nature of these biases and their implications for the results will be discussed in the context of each model.

An additional advantage to the two model approach is that it allows us to explore the sensitivity of the implied efficient solutions to various assumptions regarding costs and supply behavior. The remainder of this section describes both of the models, their implicit assumptions and solutions, the method of costing used as an input to each of the models, their results, and the overall findings for cost effective mixes of first term and career personnel for each of the occupations. Additionally, some inferences are made regarding the current mix and the stated objective force mix in the Air Force.

MODEL 1: THE SIMPLE STEADY STATE MODEL

The steady state model takes wages as given by the current wage rates and assumes that any amount of labor demanded will be available at those rates. In this system retention is assumed to be simply a function of demand bounded only by the conditions that the second term inventory of a career force cannot exceed the inventory of the first term force with an implicit retention rate of one. Under these conditions the problem is to minimize

$$W^*_f L^*_f + W_c L_c = \text{total cost} \tag{45}$$

---

[2] Although the term "wage" is used as a convenience, the fact that "cost" in the military context incorporates much beyond visible wage is fully borne in mind and explicitly addressed under "Costing" below.

subject to the production constraint:[3]

$$\overline{E} - \left(a_1^* L_f^{*\,-\rho} + a_2 L_c^{\,-\rho} \right)^{-\frac{1}{\rho}} = 0 , \tag{46}$$

where $\overline{E}$ = the effectiveness level achieved at the current first term and career input levels. In this case, the solution is found by solving

$$W_f^* - \lambda \left[\left(a_1^* L_f^{*\,-\rho} + a_2 L_c^{\,-\rho} \right)^{-\frac{1}{\rho} - 1} \left(a_1^* L_f^{*\,-\rho-1} \right) \right] = 0 ,$$

$$W_c - \lambda \left[\left(a_1^* L_f^{*\,-\rho} + a_2 L_c^{\,-\rho} \right)^{-\frac{1}{\rho} - 1} \left(a_2 L_c^{\,-\rho-1} \right) \right] = 0,$$

and

$$\overline{E} - \left[\left(a_1^* L_f^{*\,-\rho} + a_2 L_c^{\,-\rho} \right)^{-\frac{1}{\rho}} \right] = 0 .$$

The first order condition for either the first term or career input can also be written, e.g.,

$$\frac{W_c}{\left[a_1^* L_f^{*\,-\rho} + a_2 L_c^{\,-\rho} \right]^{-\frac{1}{\rho} - 1} \left(a_2 L_c^{\,-\rho-1} \right)} = \lambda .$$

The numerator represents the marginal cost of hiring an additional member of the career force, and the denominator represents the marginal productivity. Since the ratio of marginal cost to marginal productivity must equal the Lagrangian multiplier λ, the ratio must be the same for both first term and career personnel. Thus, for the two experience categories, the ratio of their marginal costs must equal the ratio of their marginal products to minimize costs at a constant effectiveness level.[4]

---

[3] Recall that L_f^* is an index of first term labor deriving from the first tier of the productivity model. W_f^* is the per unit cost of L_f^* and is computed as $W_f^* = W_f L_f / L_f^*$. Although the real expression we wish to minimize is $W_f L_f + W_c L_c$, it is easily demonstrated that, in a steady state, minimizing $W_f^* L_f^* + W_c L_c$, in fact, minimizes $W_f L_f + W_c L_c$.

[4] Having solved for L_f^* and L_c analytically, an actual cost minimizing first term inventory L_f can be derived from the first tier aggregation function and specified continuation rates. In this manner attrition and training pipeline factors can be taken into account. For example, for any given occupation, the first term inventory L_f is composed of both a series of on-the-job experience categories L_{fi} and a category for first termers not yet on the job, hence, not in the training pipeline. Thus, $L_f = L_{fi} + L_{fp}$. For the purposes of this analysis we have taken the service attrition goals and the current training pipeline proportions as fixed and have thus apportioned first term personnel across the L_{fi} and L_{fp} categories accordingly. In this way efficient units of L_f are converted into actual inventories of L_{fi} and L_{fp} and hence an overall first term inventory L_f.

Although this model is unrealistic with respect to the retention of additional career personnel (i.e., by implicitly assuming that a retention rate of one can be had at the current wage), it does provide conservative estimates with respect to cases where either a retention of the current mix or a more junior mix is indicated, since additional career inputs are systematically underpriced and hence overestimated in terms of cost effectiveness. Furthermore, this model provides useful upperbound estimates of career inventories in a cost minimizing context for cases where more career inputs appear cost effective. For example, consider a case where in the context of the unconstrained model a slightly more career intensive force is indicated and where in the context of the constrained model the indication is that these additional career inputs cannot be purchased cost effectively. In this case, it may well be that a small expansion of the eligible force for reenlistment may be sufficient to attract the indicated small number of additional reenlistments at no increase in wage. Thus, although the unconstrained model is biased with respect to estimates of cost effective mixes which indicate a substantial increase in career inputs, it may not be biased with respect to the cost effectiveness of small changes toward a more senior force.

MODEL 2: THE SUPPLY CONSTRAINED MODEL

The supply constrained model goes one step further than the simple steady state framework in modeling the military labor system, inasmuch as it incorporates the fact that the military must pay a wage differential—typically reenlistment bonuses—to induce the retention of additional career personnel. In this context, career wage, like the first term and career inventory, is a variable in the system.[5]

In this case, retention is not only a variable function of first term labor but also of the career wage. For the purposes of this analysis we have selected a supply function which is at once sufficiently sophisticated to be consistent with the findings of the empirical work on military retention and at the same time sufficiently simple so as to provide an analytic solution to the constrained optimization problem. Specifically, the supply function selection is of the form

$$L_c = L^*_f \, bW_c^2 \, ,$$

where the derivative of career labor with respect to career wage is equal to

$$\frac{dL_c}{dW_c} = 2L^*_f \, bW_c \, ,$$

and where the elasticity of supply is given by

$$\frac{W_c}{L_c} \, \frac{dL_2}{dW_c} = 2 \, .$$

[5] It should be noted that for the current analysis the supply of first term labor is unconstrained. This assumption will tend to bias the results in favor of first term labor for those cases where although the

This function is a positively sloped quadratic function which, for a specified level of L^*_f, reflects a positive relationship between career wage and first term retention. Thus, higher levels of retention require increases in career wage. For each occupation in the sample the parameters of the supply function are estimated to reflect the current retention conditions for that occupation. Enhanced retention and, in turn, increased career wage represent departures from the current occupationally specific retention conditions. For purposes of this analysis we have fixed the limiting value of L^*_f in the supply model at $4L^*_f$ for any starting value of L^*_f and hence have determined a retention rate of one as the limit for any particular specification.

This particular functional form is similar in many respects to the class of supply functions which have typically been applied to the problem of supply analysis in the military context.[6] The advantage of this particular formulation lies in both its mathematical tractability and the reasonableness of its shape. Furthermore, this function is a constant elasticity of supply function, and that elasticity is equal to 2. This is an important attribute of the function since the results of research efforts regarding the elasticity of supply for the first reenlistment decision indicate that the elasticity is approximately equal to 2.[7] Thus, this formulation of the supply function is not only consistent with the empirical literature on military supply behavior and the theoretical literature on functional forms for supply analysis, but also greatly simplifies the difficult problem of finding an analytic solution to the set of nonlinear first-order conditions needed for optimization.[8]

The set of efficient mixes of first term and career labor that solve this particular model will be conservative with respect to the utilization of additional career labor since, as structured, this model regards the military employer as a monopsonist with respect to career labor—that is, an employer who unlike the normal competitive employer faces an upward sloping supply curve. The effect of the monopsony conditions are that the military will pay a higher price for career labor (the margin-

---

current supply of first term labor is sufficient to meet current demands, a shift in demand indicated by the unconstrained optimization may not be feasible given current wage rates.

Consider the supply function which the military as a competitive firm currently faces with respect to all first term labor reflected by Curve A in Fig. 3. Here we see the supply curve as flat for the current wage rates and upward sloping thereafter. If demand Curve B represents current occupational demand for first term labor it is clear that there is an adequate supply at the current wage rate W^*_f. If, however, the results of unconstrained optimization indicate a shift in first term demand to, say, Curve C, then at the current wage rate supply will be inadequate to meet the new demand. In order to integrate this constraint into the current framework we would need to know not only the general supply conditions (i.e. first term elasticities of supply), but also the particular supply and demand conditions for each occupation.

Furthermore, in the context of a declining manpower pool in the 1980s, this problem is likely to be exacerbated for each occupation as the overall supply curve will shift to the left, making fewer accessions feasible at current wage rates.

[6] Specifically, the classes of functions that have been applied to supply analysis include the exponential (Jacquette and Nelson, 1974); lognormal and the logistic (Fisher, 1969, and Grissmer et al., 1972).

[7] Gates et al. (1970) and Enns (1975).

[8] The predominant disadvantage of this particular function derives from the fact that if both L^*_f and L_c are allowed to vary, the resultant cost function $w^*_f L^*_f + (4L_f^* b)^{-.5} \times L_c^{1.5} = \text{Cost}$ is convex to the origin as opposed to the normal linear or concave shape and does not guarantee an efficient solution. Figure 4 illustrates the relationships. The production constraint is represented by the curve E. Curves A and B represent linear and non-linear concave cost curves and Curve C represents the non-linear convex case. It can be seen that while the more normal cost curves (A&B) provide cost minimizing tangencies for the production constraint, Curve C does not provide a true minimum value. In fact, such cost curves may generate more than one intersection or none at all. For purposes of this analysis we have held L^*_f constant for each occupation in the supply function, thereby creating a cost function which is of the more normal concave shape. The effect of this restriction is to understate required amounts of wage increase to induce additional career labor; however, within the relevant range of consideration, this effect can be easily shown to be trivial.

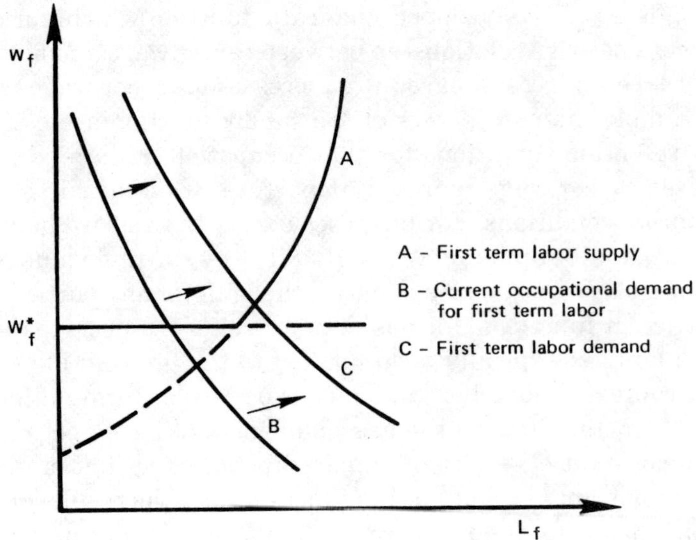

Fig. 3—Supply and demand of first term labor

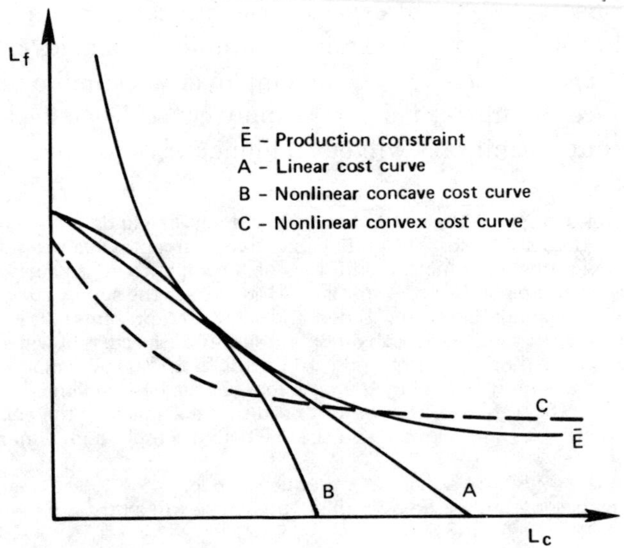

Fig. 4—Relationship of cost curves and production constraint

al cost as opposed to the average cost in the competitive framework) and, hence, will use it less intensely than in the competitive market. Furthermore, we have ignored the potential for cross training in the system. This is a process whereby individuals who complete one term of service in a particular occupation, reenlist for a different occupation. In this way career resources can be transferred from an occupation that may have a surplus of potential reenlistees to an occupation that has difficulty in meeting career requirements. Although such cross trainees induce additional training costs, additional bonus costs may be avoided as well as certain attrition costs, since the proportion of cross trainees who fail to complete a second term of service is extremely small. The specific solution to the cost minimizing conditions in this case is found by solving:

$$W_f^* - \lambda \left[\left(a_1^* L_f^{*-\rho} + a_2 L_c^{-\rho} \right)^{-\frac{1}{\rho}-1} \left(a_1^* L_f^{*-\rho-1} \right) \right] = 0$$

and

$$1.5Kb^{-1.5} L_c^{.5} - \lambda \left[\left(a_1^* L_f^{*-\rho} + a_2 L_c^{-\rho} \right)^{-\frac{1}{\rho}-1} \left(a_2 L_c^{-\rho-1} \right) \right] = 0.$$

and

$$E - \left[a_1^* L_f^{*-\rho} + a_2 L_c^{-\rho} \right]^{-\frac{1}{\rho}} = 0$$

Note that the value of $4L_f^*$ in the supply function has been fixed at K and hence is treated as a constant in the model.

COSTING

Before turning to the results of the optimization models it is important that basic cost issues be briefly considered.[9] As previously mentioned, the appropriate concept in measuring the cost of additional first term and career personnel is the average marginal cost. The specific costing technique consists of averaging cost elements for each year of service over each of the years included in the first term

[9] A full discussion of cost and cost elements is contained in Appendix B.

and second and subsequent terms of service. This valuation, which includes all pay and benefits received on an annual basis, as well as annualized values for such important cost elements as training and accession costs and retirement (for example, at say 20 years of service), is distributed equally across each of the career years of service up to that point. Table 13 summarizes the cost elements derived from this technique for one occupation in the sample, the 306X0 cryptographic equipment repair specialty.

In terms of relative costs, we can see in Table 13 the impact of each cost element on overall cost. For example, if we use as the measure of relative costs the value of pay and allowances alone, we find that first term cost is 65.3 percent of career cost. If we include the cost of retirement to pay and allowances, we find that first term costs are reduced to 52.5 percent of career cost. In the case of the AFSC 306X0, we find that the addition of training costs to the previous calculation increases first term costs to 74.7 percent of career costs.

Thus, the costs of training and retirement substantially alter the relative costs of first term and career personnel for each occupation. They are thus extremely important in determining efficient allocations of first term and career personnel. In contrast, however, removing the bonus considerations in the career cost estimate in each of the calculations only raises the relative cost of first term personnel by less than 3 percent in each case. Clearly, the results are sensitive to estimates of training and retirement costs and if either of those costs changes substantially, the results of the models will also change.

NUMERICAL RESULTS

The numerical results developed for each of the optimization models are based on the constant elasticity of substitution productivity functions described in Section III and the cost data summarized above. The results reflect the analytically determined least costly combinations of first term and career inputs at constant effectiveness levels consistent with the assumptions of each model.

As an overview to an analysis of the specific results of each of the models, Fig. 5 shows the likely implications of each model in terms of impact on cost minimizing labor allocations. First term and career labor are represented by L_f and L_c respectively. Productivity is represented by a constant level of effectiveness constraint, the curve $\bar{E}$. Both of the costing and supply models are represented by a particular isocost curve derived from the cost function each entails. Curve A corresponds to the simple steady state model and is tangent to the production constraint at point (L_{cA}, L_{fA}). If we take the point $(L^*_c \, L^*_f)$ as the current inventory, it is clear that the implication of applying the simple competitive model is that a shift in resources toward a more senior force would be cost effective. The supply constrained model is represented by the Curve B. In this case the resultant cost curve is nonlinear, reflecting the fact that career wage is not held constant and hence the ratio of first term to career wage is not constant. For increasing units of career labor more and more units of first term labor must be forgone for overall cost to remain constant. In this case we find the point of tangency to be $(L_c z \, L_f z)$ which, while entailing a much less intensive use of career labor than Case A, still indicates a more experienced force than that reflected in the initial inventory. Although these particular curves are provided simply by way of example, they do illustrate the implications

Table 13

SAMPLE COST ELEMENTS FOR AFSC (306X0)

Years of Service	Basic Pay	Reenlistment Bonuses	Quarters & Subsistence Allowances	Miscellaneous & Support	Retirement	Training & Accession	Total
1	5069	--	1229	2657	--	4296	13251
2	5579	--	1404	2598	--	4296	13817
3	6014	--	1564	3097	--	4296	14971
4	6492	--	1716	3245	--	4296	15749
5	7026	1082	1886	3418	3790	--	15202
6	7110	1082	1977	3418	3790	--	17377
7	7637	1082	2044	3418	3790	--	17971
8	7762	1082	2099	3418	3790	--	18151
9	8195	647	2162	3547	3790	--	18341
10	8305	647	2203	3547	3790	--	18492
11	8779	647	2262	3547	3790	--	19025
12	8898	647	2292	3547	3790	--	19174
13	9435	--	2234	3653	3790	--	19112
14	9625	--	2387	3653	3790	--	19455
15	10105	--	2421	3653	3790	--	19969
16	10252	--	2452	3653	3790	--	20147
17	10727	--	2489	3813	3790	--	20819
18	10908	--	2523	3813	3790	--	21034
19	11316	--	2578	3813	3790	--	21497
20	11416	--	2655	3813	3790	--	21674
30	17260	--	3031	4149	2456	--	26896

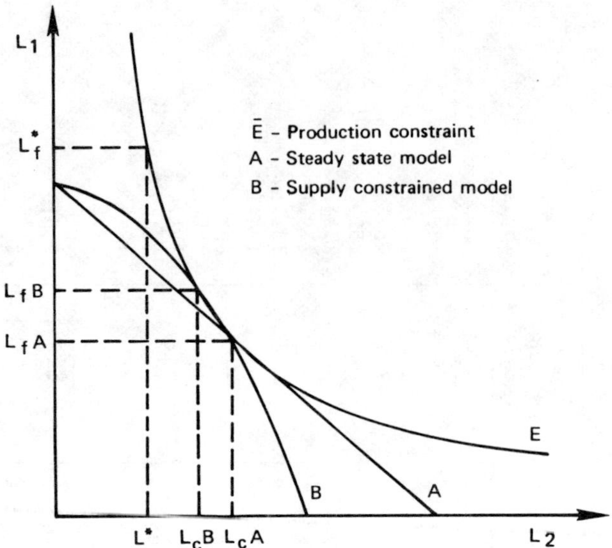

Fig. 5—Implications of cost and supply models for minimizing
costs, holding effectiveness constant

of the different assumptions implicit in each of the different models for cost minimizing solutions. In general, the simple competitive model will indicate cost minimizing mixes which are more career intensive than those indicated by the supply
constrained model.

MODEL 1 RESULTS

Table 14 reflects the results of cost minimizing optimization derived from the
simple competitive model. The current inventory and the implied efficient distribution are shown for each occupation. The results imply that a more senior force is
desirable. Overall, the current distribution for this sample of occupations is just
below 52 percent first term personnel while the implied efficient distribution for the
same sample is just less than 45 percent first term. The variance about the two
overall estimates is likewise quite different (in the current inventory the variance
is .006 while for the implied efficient solutions the variance is .028) reflecting the
fact that in the cost minimizing context, solutions are not bound by a general
tendency to balance distributions across occupations. Thus, for example, while the
general implication of the model is to reduce the first term career mix in general,
in over 40 percent of the specific cases, either an increase in first term inputs or a
retention of the current distribution is indicated. In the remaining cases it must be
borne in mind that the implicit assumptions of the simple competitive model tend
to bias the results in favor of additional career personnel, since the assumption of
unconstrained supply contradicts the empirical evidence of retention behavior.
Thus, results that indicate more intensive use of career labor reflect more upper
bounds of career content than realistic measures of optimal first term/career mixes.

Table 14

MODEL 1. SIMPLE STEADY STATE MODEL RESULTS

AFSC	Description	Current Force[a]			Implied Efficient Force		
		Percent First Term	First Term	Career	Percent First Term	First Term	Career
326X0	Avionics Aerospace Ground Equipment Specialist	53.7	570	490	26.0	232	670
326X1	Integrated Avionic Component Specialist	57.6	1023	752	37.0	578	978
326X2	Integrated Avionic Systems Specialist	57.5	1210	895	36.0	656	1164
304X4	Ground Radio Repairman	44.2	2834	3572	20.0	374	4764
306X0	Electronic Communications Equipment Repairman	40.5	1000	1472	20.0	126	1962
421X3	Aerospace Ground Equipment Repairman	58.6	4228	2989	33.0	1998	4074
422X1	Aircraft Environmental Systems Repairman	56.1	1141	892	45.0	854	1050
431X1	Aircraft Maintenance Specialist	48.3	21331	22828	45.0	19301	23961
542X0	Electrician	46.2	836	907	52.0	914	858
543X0	Electrical Power Production Specialist	48.3	1433	1537	33.0	918	1833
571X0	Fire Protection Specialist	62.0	3899	2385	38.0	2075	3351
622X0	Cook	41.1	1724	2473	60.0	2758	1803
631X0	Fuels Specialist	38.4	2349	3766	83.0	6076	1257
647X0	Materials Facility Specialist	48.6	4049	4278	48.0	3987	4310
671X3	Accounting Specialist	51.4	1733	1637	68.0	2453	1175
902X0	Hospital Corpsman	59.8	4430	2980	59.0	4300	2988
971X0	Dental Specialist	65.0	1403	755	64.0	1367	780

[a]SOURCE: MRA&L (MPP)

As anticipated, those occupations associated with substantial training costs are also associated with the cost minimizing solutions that entail the most intensive use of career labor. Similarly, those occupations in the medium or low skill category entail the most intensive use of first term labor in the cost minimizing context.

In general, the findings derived from the simple competitive model are conservative with respect to cases where a more first term intensive force is indicated, or where the current mix is found to be the efficient one, and are biased with respect to cases where more career personnel are indicated. For those cases the results should be regarded as upper bounds only.

MODEL 2 RESULTS AND COMPOSITE FINDINGS

Table 15 summarizes the results of the supply constrained model as applied to those occupations for which in the context of the simple competitive model, additional career personnel are indicated as cost effective. For the remainder of the cases composite findings are reported which reflect the results of the first model. In sum, these results reflect the single best estimates for each occupation and are presented as a summary for the modeling exercise.[10]

As anticipated, constraining the supply of personnel into the career force on the determination of cost effective combinations of first term and career personnel substantially reduces the size of the efficient career content. For example, the results of the competitive model indicate that, on average, career content should be increased by almost 25 percent in those occupations where additional career personnel are cost effective at the current wage. For the same occupations, however, the results of the supply constrained model indicate that, on average, the career content should be increased by little more than 7 percent. The specific magnitude of change from one context to the other for any given occupation will, of course, depend on a variety of factors, including the first term wage, the current mix of first term and career personnel, and the parameters of the productivity model. Thus, these estimates will vary from occupation to occupation. Nevertheless, the overriding result of the supply constraint is to significantly reduce career cost effectiveness for each occupation considered. Assumptions regarding supply must therefore be regarded as a critical element of the determination of efficient force structures.

An additional product of the supply constrained model is an estimate of the average marginal career wage required to induce the efficient number of career personnel in each occupation. To put the resultant values in context, consider that the average marginal cost of career labor without a reenlistment bonus is estimated at \$18,907, and with a level two reenlistment bonus at \$19,275. In each case where additional career personnel are indicated, the resultant estimate of the optimal average marginal career wage falls well within the bounds of the current bonus structure.

---

[10] These results are presented as *estimates* based on the assumptions implicit in the general framework and the specific assumptions of each model. They are not necessarily true optimal values of first term/career distributions because many dynamic considerations are ignored and important factors such as attrition, enlisted supply, and eligibility for reenlistment are only estimated values from current experience. Changes in these factors may substantially alter the findings.

Table 15

SUPPLY CONSTRAINED MODEL AND COMPOSITE RESULTS

AFSC		Current Force			Implied Efficient Force			
		Percent First Term	First Term	Career	Percent First Term	First Term	Career	Average Marginal Career Costs
326X0	Avionics Aerospace Ground Equipment Specialist	53.7	570	490	48.0	497	522	19514
326X1	Integrated Avionic Component Specialist	57.6	1023	752	41.0	628	925	19500
326X2	Integrated Avionic Systems Specialist	57.5	1210	895	49.0	960	987	19700
304X4	Ground Radio Repairman	44.2	2834	3572	40.0	2492	3714	19278
306X0	Electronic Communications Equipment Repairman	40.5	1000	1472	36.0	865	1562	19105
421X3	Aerospace Ground Equipment Repairman	58.6	4228	2989	36.0	2186	3960	19803
422X1	Aircraft Environmental Systems Repairman	56.1	1141	892	55.0	1094	845	--
431X1	Aircraft Maintenance Specialist	48.3	21331	22828	45.0	19301	23961	--
542X0	Electrician	46.2	836	907	52.0	914	858	--
543X0	Electrical Power Production Specialist	48.3	1423	1537	48.0	1425	1545	--
571X0	Fire Protection Specialist	62.0	3899	2385	44.0	2427	3148	19200
622X0	Cook	41.1	1724	2473	60.0	2758	1803	--
631X0	Fuels Specialist	38.4	2349	3766	83.0	6076	1257	--
647X0	Materials Facility Specialist	48.6	4049	4278	48.0	3987	4310	--
671X3	Accounting Specialist	57.4	1733	1637	68.0	2453	1175	--
902X0	Hospital Corpsman	59.8	4430	2980	59.0	4300	2988	--
981X0	Dental Specialist	65.0	1430	755	64.0	1367	780	--

In general, the findings for the sample of occupations included in the study indicate that, in the aggregate, the current first term/career inventory is very close to the one that would be selected on the basis of cost minimizing criteria. For example, the proportion of first term personnel in the current force is roughly 50 percent; the proportion in the cost effective force is 49 percent. In terms of overall force size, the current force is only slightly more than 1.5 percent larger than the implied efficient force, and the career content not even a percent lower. On the basis of aggregate measures alone, it would seem that the current force structure is very close to a cost minimizing structure. However, when the results are disaggregated by occupational specialty, we find a great deal of variance between the current and implied efficient distributions—variance that has important cost consequences.

In Table 15 we see that in 40 percent of the cases more first term personnel are indicated than in the current distribution, and in over 50 percent of the cases more career personnel are indicated. In only about 10 percent of the cases do we find that the current distribution of personnel is essentially the same as the implied efficient distribution. The tendency of these discrepancies is, as one would anticipate, toward more intensive use of career personnel in highly skilled occupations and increased use of first term personnel in lower skilled occupations, and, in general, more variance among occupations than in the current force structure.

Figure 6 shows the relationship between differences in the current and implied efficient occupational force structures and occupational skill level, represented by length of formal training. Differences in force structure are summarized as the ratio of the proportion of first term personnel in the current force to the proportion of first term personnel in the implied efficient occupational forces. When this ratio is greater than one, the current force is more first term intensive than is the implied efficient force and, conversely, when this ratio is less than one the current force is more career intensive than is the implied efficient force. We find that for occupations with more than three months of formal training, the implied efficient force is more career intensive than the current force, indicating a cost effective shift of resources toward greater numbers of career personnel. Conversely, for occupations with less than three months of formal training, the implied efficient force is either the same as the current force or more first term intensive, indicating a cost effective move to a more junior force. The implied efficient first term proportions for the three most skilled occupations in the sample are only slightly lower than the current proportions. This result is indicative of the imposition of the supply constraint in these cases and the fact that these occupations currently have relatively high career proportions (almost 60 percent in each of the cases). Nevertheless, for this set of occupational specialties, high skill occupations seem to be systematically underrepresented by career personnel, and low skill specialties appear to be systematically underrepresented by first term personnel.

The cost implications of these differences are significant. A comparison of the total force cost of the current force and the implied efficient force indicates that at current effectiveness levels and at essentially the same total force size, a redistribution of first term/career pesonnel within occupations subject to constant total force proportions is associated with a net savings of almost $18 million. Naturally, these costs are subject to change depending on the validity of the assumptions; however, they do underscore the important potential cost consequences of differing the mix of first term and career personnel within occupations over a fixed force mix, and

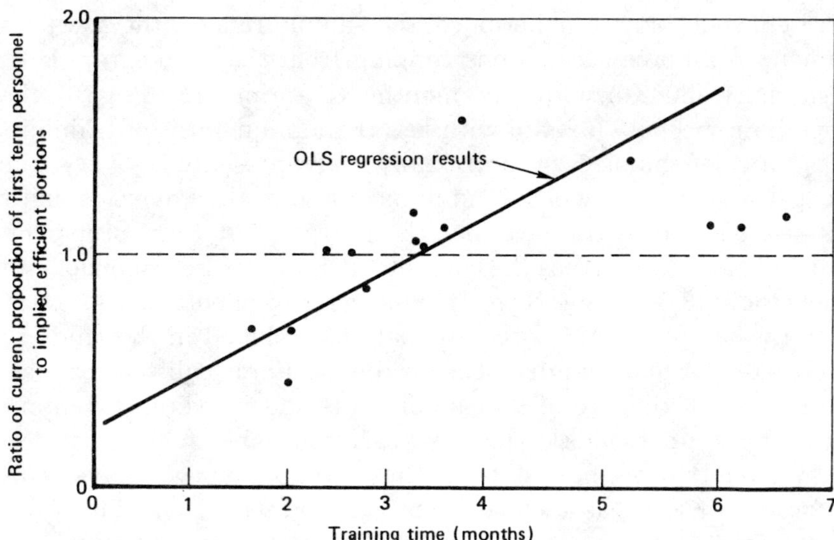

Fig. 6—Relationship between specialty skill level and variation
between current and implied efficient specialty structures

emphasize the importance of deriving cost effective overall force structures from
individual occupational analysis.

From the results of the model, we conclude that while in the aggregate the
current distribution of first term and career personnel for these occupational specialties seems to be quite close to an efficient distribution, the distributions within
many of the individual occupations are not. The findings presented here tend to
indicate an overutilization of career personnel in many medium and low skill
occupations and an underutilization of career personnel in high skill occupations.
Furthermore, these results indicate that the reenlistment bonus is not used to full
advantage in this set of occupations, since the current bonus distribution includes
only one member of the sample whereas the results of this analysis indicate that
reenlistment bonuses could be cost effectively applied in at least seven cases. Finally, the findings of this analysis strongly emphasize the importance of determining
overall force structures from individual occupational analysis, as opposed to determining force structures exclusively in the aggregate.

FORCE-WIDE IMPLICATIONS AND THE CURRENT OBJECTIVE FORCE STRUCTURE

Although the specific conclusions to be drawn from the results of this analysis
apply exclusively to the sample of occupations included in the study, on the basis
of the size of the sample and its representativeness certain inferences regarding the
Air Force enlisted force as a whole can be made. For example, although the sample
of occupations included in the study represent only a small fraction of the total
number of Air Force occupational specialties, the total inventory of enlisted personnel included in the sampled occupations constitutes almost 25 percent of the entire

Air Force enlisted force. Furthermore, the sample reflects the spectrum of skill levels among Air Force occupations ranging from the cryptographic equipment repair specialty (306X0) with six months of formal training to the vehicle driver-operator specialty (622X0) with less than two months of training. The fact that this particular sample is proportionally overrepresented by very high and low skill occupations—both of which tend to have higher than average first term proportions—is reflected in the fact that the current first term proportion for the sample is 51.5 percent whereas the current Air Force wide proportion of first term personnel is only 48.6 percent. Nevertheless, in terms of both absolute size and skill variation, the sample of Air Force occupations included in the study provides a reasonable basis for making inferences for the Air Force enlisted force as a whole.

On the basis of the size of the sample in terms of overall inventory and the distribution by occupational skill level, we can reasonably infer that the conclusions that follow from the specific results for those occupations will have general applications for the Air Force as a whole. Thus, it would seem that an overall Air Force proportion of first term to career personnel of around 50 percent at current strength levels would be consistent with cost minimizing criteria, and that a retention of the current enlisted force mix of roughly 49 percent is desirable. Furthermore, for many occupations in this sample, the specific first term/career mixes do not necessarily represent cost effective mixes. Specifically, it is likely that for many high skill occupations, career personnel are underutilized and that for many low skill occupations first term personnel are underutilized. In general, however, this research indicates that the Air Force enlisted force as currently constituted represents a reasonably cost effective distribution of personnel in terms of first term and career inputs. However, when the results of this research are compared with the stated Air Force enlisted goals, substantial differences appear.

Table 16 represents a comparison of the implied efficient distributions of first term and career personnel from this analysis and the current goals for force distribution set by the Air Force represented by the currently stated force "objectives." In this case the differences are striking. Overall, the implied efficient distribution indicates about a 51 percent proportion of first term personnel, whereas the objective force goal is for an overall proportion of almost 67 percent for these occupations. Furthermore, although the general tendency of the objective distributions is consistent with that of the implied efficient ones—namely, that higher skill occupations are indicated to have a less predominantly junior force than lower skill occupations do—the magnitudes of the differences and the absolute proportions are substantial. For example, in none of the occupational groupings in the objective force does less than 56 percent of the force consist of first term personnel. In the implied efficient context over half the cases indicated a less than 50 percent proportion of first term personnel. What is more important is to consider that the total force size is held relatively constant across both force structures. The implied efficient force which tends to indicate a maintenance of the current force size (i.e., close to 500,000 enlisted personnel) is almost identical to the force size reflected in the objective force structure, again close to 500,000 enlisted personnel. Without regard to cost effectiveness, the productivity analysis indicates that moving from a 50/50 mix to a 67/33 mix cannot be achieved if effectiveness levels are to be maintained without an overall increase in the force size. Apparently the objectives set by the Air Force are not a cost minimizing force structure, and the objective

Table 16

OBJECTIVE FORCE AND IMPLIED EFFICIENT FORCE

AFSC	Description	Percent First Term	First Term	Career	Percent First Term	First Term	Career
326X0	Avionics Aerospace Ground Equipment Specialist	62	3080	1914	48	497	522
326X1	Integrated Avionic Component Specialist	62	3080	1914	41	628	925
326X2	Integrated Avionic Systems Specialist	62	3080	1914	49	960	987
304X4[a]	Ground Radio Repairman	56	7176	5726	40	2492	3714
306X0[a]	Electronic Communications Equipment Repairman	68	3519	1654	36	865	1562
421X3	Aerospace Ground Equipment Repairman	67	13764	6549	36	2186	3960
422X1	Aircraft Environmental Systems Repairman	67	13764	6549	55	1094	845
431X1[a]	Aircraft Maintenance Specialist	60	29145	19202	45	19301	23961
542X0[a]	Electrician	68	1894	895	52	914	858
543X0[a]	Electrical Power Production Specialist	73	2210	840	48	1425	1545
571X0[a]	Fire Protection Specialist	79	5271	1444	44	2427	3148
622X0[a]	Cook	71	3976	1631	60	2758	1803
631X0[a]	Fuels Specialist	79	5678	1528	83	6076	1257
647X0	Materials Facility Specialist	65	18278	10051	48	3987	4310
671X0[a]	Accounting Specialist	63	3737	2189	68	2453	1175
902X0	Hospital Corpsman	66	8584	4542	59	4300	2988
981X1[a]	Dental Specialist	67	1884	906	64	1367	780

SOURCE: Air Force Personnel Plan, March 1977.

[a]This AFSC is the sole member of the Career Progression Group, or the predominant occupation in the CPG.

force may entail actual reductions in overall effectiveness levels. This suggests that from a policy perspective, the problem is not so much with the current distribution of personnel, but with the stated objectives for force distribution which the Air Force seeks to achieve. This analysis indicates that the currently planned redistribution of personnel toward the stated objectives may not be cost effective and that these objectives may actually entail reductions in total force capability.

In summary, this section has indicated the importance of productivity considerations for the development of estimates of cost effective mixes of first term and career personnel. To this end, two simple models were developed, each of which served to integrate the productivity findings of the previous section with various cost and supply considerations relevant to the military labor context. Although the specific cost estimates and supply assumptions reflect accurate and reasonable representations of that environment, the specific results of the analysis are not intended as specific point estimates of optimal first term and career mixes, but rather as feasible spaces of force distribution consistent with general notions of cost effectiveness. The general findings of the analysis indicate that the current distribution of first term and career personnel in the Air Force, in the aggregate, is consistent with distributions that are cost effective. With respect to specific occupations the findings indicate that, in general, low skill occupations tend to underutilize first term labor and that high skill occupations tend to underutilize career labor. Furthermore, it is noted that the reenlistment bonus is not used cost effectively in the sample of occupations included in the study, specifically that for this sample of occupations more bonuses are indicated especially in high skill occupations. Finally, a comparison of the implied efficient distributions with the objective distributions set by the Air Force suggests that the objectives are substantially overrepresented by first term personnel. The results of the productivity analysis demonstrate that attainment of the objective force cannot be achieved without substantial increases in overall force size if effectiveness is to remain constant.

VII. CONCLUSIONS, EXTENSIONS, AND POLICY RECOMMENDATIONS

Although the theoretical relationships between labor cost and productivity in the context of economic efficiency have long been understood, the difficult problem of actually measuring and evaluating the contribution of specific labor categories to the production of military effectiveness has received relatively little attention. As a result, economically efficient allocations of manpower resources have neither been rigorously determined nor even approximated with much confidence.

One of the most important dimensions of this complex allocation problem is the distribution of enlisted personnel by length of service, summarized by the mix of first term and career personnel. The specific objective of this research has been to provide empirical estimates of the substitution potential between first term and career personnel for a sample of Air Force occupational specialties. The importance of these estimates for the overall allocation problem has been demonstrated by optimization analyses conducted for each of the occupations in the sample. Although the particular cost and supply assumptions implicit in the optimization model are reasonable, the results of the analysis are not intended as definitive point estimates of optimal first term and career mixes. Rather they are reflections of the feasible spaces of force distribution consistent with the general criteria of cost effectiveness.

Thus, the conclusions of the research do not suggest nor are they intended to suggest extensive policy changes, although important findings with policy relevance can be derived from the research. They relate to (1) the general problem of measuring and evaluating the productivity of labor in the military (non-market) environment; (2) the problem of determining economically efficient allocations of manpower resources given specific information regarding productivity; and (3) the specific problem of estimating economically efficient distributions of manpower resources given the supply and demand conditions of the sample of occupations included in the study.

LABOR PRODUCTIVITY IN THE MILITARY ENVIRONMENT

The findings indicate that the potential for substitution between first term and career labor within particular occupations is significant but not unlimited. That is to say, we have found that the elasticity of substitution between first term and career personnel within particular occupations is neither zero, indicating no substitution potential, nor infinite, indicating an unlimited substitution potential. We have found that productivity is positively related to experience and that both the substitution potential and the relative productivity of experience categories are related to occupational skill level. Specifically, we have found that more technically demanding occupations tend to be associated with both higher marginal rates of substitution between first term and career labor, reflecting the length of time required to become job skill proficient and lower elasticities of substitution, indicating rigidity in the requirement for high experience personnel.

With respect to the measurement of labor productivity in the military environment we have found that estimates of military labor productivity derived from a supervisor's subjective assessments can be useful and accurate measures when designed, administered, and analyzed with care and planning. Given the advantages of cost and potential sample size, the survey approach of estimating the productivity of various military labor categories may, in fact, be the best method of providing these measures for the purpose of policy planning.

Finally, we conclude that the constant elasticity of substitution formulation of the military labor aggregation function is a useful reflection of production reality. Specifically we have found that the CES formulation is superior to either of the two most commonly used formulations, the linear aggregation function and the Cobb-Douglas formulation.

It should be kept in mind that the specific results presented here apply exclusively to the sample of occupations included in the Enlisted Utilization Survey data base, which were selected on the basis of their size and representativeness in terms of overall skill distributions. Because of the selection criteria of large overall size and large individual work units, the estimates of substitution potential derived for this specific sample of occupations are likely to be both technically and mission feasible. For example, the frequency distributions of first current term/career mixes within specific work units presented in Section II for several of the occupations in the sample indicate that a high enough variation exists in first term/career mixes across the large work units to make substitutions that are technically feasible and practical in the context of mission requirements. Clearly, an important extension of the research would be to explore the kinds of productivity relationships contained in this research for occupational specialties which may not be either as large, in general, or as large in terms of unit composition as the occupations included in this sample. In these cases the relationship between economically desirable substitutions and substitutions that are practical in the overall mission context can be explored. This relationship is likely to be important in the Army and Navy where mission requirements in terms of work unit size entail a great deal more decentralization than in the Air Force.

With respect to the productivity analysis itself, the most promising extensions of this research would be ones that explore other important elements of overall efficient distributions of enlisted manpower resources. Such extensions might include analyses of marginal rates and elasticities of substitution between other categories of labor such as those disaggregated by mental category, previous work, or educational experience. The approach adopted here might be extended to determining cross elasticities of substitution among occupational specialties for the purpose of aiding manpower planners in the design of relevant occupational groupings and the design of training courses for those occupations. Cross elasticities of substitution for various occupations summarize the substitution potential of personnel in one occupation for another. Thus, the greater the potential for substituting one type of personnel for another (i.e., the greater the homogeneity of the two labor types) the more reasonable it would be to combine the two types of labor into a single category. Furthermore, analysis of this kind could serve to identify asymmetries in cross elasticities of substitution where substitution may be relatively easy in one direction, say from a more technical to a less technical field, and quite difficult in the opposite direction. Such analysis would aid in the determination of force readiness and surge capacities in time of war, by indicating the ability of a given force to meet the immediate requirements of crisis or conflict.

The policy recommendations that follow from the productivity analysis concern an expansion of current service capabilities for determining production alternatives either by exploring technically feasible combinations experimentally or by using current variations in production to indicate feasible alternatives. This capability could be expanded either (1) by research initiatives or (2) by giving the requirements determination organizations a larger role in the services which would include (a) determining manning levels and manhour requirements by occupation or mission as well as (b) determining production alternatives at different overall manning levels and different manhour requirements. In many regards the latter is preferable to the former inasmuch as organizations currently tasked with manpower rquirements determination are likely to be better able to combine the criteria of technical feasibility and mission constraints. The key, however, is the creation of proper incentives and the provision of necessary resources for these organizations to take on the expanded role. Without proper guidance and incentives, it is likely that either no new information or incomplete information would be generated. In sum, more information regarding production and labor productivity is required. This research has demonstrated one method of measuring and evaluating labor productivity in the military context and thus indicates the potential for obtaining accurate and useful demand-related information within reasonable cost and analytic bounds.

THE ECONOMICALLY EFFICIENT DISTRIBUTION OF MANPOWER RESOURCES BY LENGTH OF SERVICE

The significance and utility of the productivity estimates presented in this research have been demonstrated in the context of optimization analyses conducted for each of the occupations in the sample. The findings of the optimization analyses indicate that for the sample of occupations included in the study, the current overall mix of first term and career personnel falls within the range that would be selected on the basis of economic efficiency. However, although the distribution of personnel for the sample of specialties taken in the aggregate is consistent with cost effectiveness considerations, the distributions within specific occupations are not. Specifically, the results of the optimization analysis indicate that, in general, higher skill occupations tend to overutilize first term labor inputs and lower skill occupations tend to underutilize first term inputs.

The differences between the current distributions within the set of occupations included in the study and the implied efficient distributions have important cost consequences. The results of this analysis indicate that a redistribution of existing first term and career resources within the set of occupations analyzed would be associated with almost a $20 million cost savings and no loss in overall effectiveness. If these results were generalizable to all occupations in the Air Force, savings might exceed $100 million, and this with less than a 1 percent change in overall end strengths and less than a 3.5 percent increase in the career force. The important conclusion to be drawn from this is that aggregate estimates of efficient distributions of manpower resources must derive from the particular supply and demand conditions of the separate occupations subgroups, since distributions which appear to be consistent with cost effectiveness criteria at the aggregate level—but are not at the occupational level—are not cost effective.

Unlike the comparison between the current distribution and the implied efficient distribution, the comparison between (1) the implied efficient distribution of enlisted personnel by occupation and (2) the objective force distribution by occupation set by the Air Force as force structure goals, reveals substantial differences. In the aggregate the objective force structure for the set of occupations in the sample consists of 67 percent first term personnel and 33 percent career personnel. The implied efficient distributions in the aggregate indicate a slightly less than 50 percent first term force. Holding cost considerations aside, the fact that the objective force end strength is approximately equal to the current strength suggests that the attainment of objective force goals would be associated with a substantial reduction in overall effectiveness. That is to say, on the basis of this analysis, there is reason to believe that the objective force structure proposed by the Air Force may not be technically feasible at current effectiveness levels. Thus, whatever cost savings might be associated with moving to the objective force will be offset by reductions in actual capabilities. The findings presented here indicate that the realization of substantial cost savings need not entail a loss in effectiveness; however, these savings must derive from force structures determined by an analysis of both cost and productivity.

To reiterate, the findings presented here are not definitive; they do not represent actual optimal distributions of first term and career personnel. In order for such results to be developed additional research is required. Probably the most urgently required are analyses of the supply of enlistments and reenlistments. Although much research has already been conducted with respect to this difficult problem, additional work is necessary to more accurately reflect supply behavior in the military context, in terms of specifying technical supply relationships (i.e., the elasticities of supply with respect to wage) disaggregated by occupational groupings, and the potential for increased supply attributable to expanding pools of eligibility and more aggressive pursuit of cross training alternatives.

Furthermore, additional research is required with respect to the impact of changes in grade structure and promotion opportunity on retention rates. Although reduced promotion opportunity will probably be associated with some decline in reenlistments, the magnitudes of such changes are largely unknown. In short, the results of this research indicate that among cost considerations none is more important and more poorly understood than the costs of military labor supply at the enlistment and the first reenlistment point.

For the purposes of this analysis we have taken important elements of the current retirement and training programs as given and fixed. Changes in either the retirement program or in the mix of formal and on-the-job training would clearly have important implications for the findings of the research. For example, moving to a more senior force would have the effect, all other things being equal, of raising the level of first term productivity relative to career productivity. It would also change the desirability of alternative training strategies. Increasing the level of first term performance might well induce reductions in the amount of formal training and increases in the use of on-the-job training. The net effect of these changes might be to reduce first term training costs; hence first term relative productivity would rise and the cost of first term personnel might drop.

From a policy perspective the findings of the optimization analysis indicate that the current mix of first term and career personnel in the Air Force enlisted force is close to the mix one would have selected on the basis of cost effectiveness criteria alone. This suggests that the Air Force should be encouraged to maintain the current force structure in the aggregate. With respect to the specific allocations within occupational specialties, however, the findings indicate that a redistribution of manpower resources toward a more senior force in high skill occupations and toward a more junior force in lower skill occupations would be cost effective, despite the fact that reenlistment bonuses may be required to retain additional career personnel in high skill occupations. More importantly, the objective force structure for the Air Force varies substantially from what appears to be the economically efficient distribution of enlisted personnel by length of service with the consequence that overall effectiveness may decline. Such objective structures should be reevaluated in the light of the findings presented here in terms of introducing additional productivity considerations into the force planning process.

THE ROLE OF OSD IN FORCE STRUCTURE PLANNING

The complex problem of determining the distribution of enlisted personnel by length of service is one of the more important policy decisions the services face. This problem affects such important policy issues as procurement, attrition, retention, grade structure, and retirement. Our research has focused on a part of the policy problem—the economically efficient allocation of manpower resources—and in particular on the role of labor productivity measurement and analysis in the determination of economically efficient allocations. OSD will determine the importance of economic efficiency in the context of such other important issues as mobilization, readiness, and reserve policies—all of which are related to the issue of force distributions by length of service. In this regard the role of OSD in the determination process is one of providing guidance and incentives to each of the services for making economically efficient allocations of manpower resources. OSD cannot make such determinations for the services nor should it adopt that position. What can be done, however, is to demonstrate general approaches and methodologies to the service in answer to important resource allocation questions and to pursue the guidance with specific incentives for expanding current capabilities. For example, the recent consolidation of the Personnel and Manpower directorates in the Air Force is a promising sign for the efficient allocation of manpower resources, since the sources of supply and demand information will now be integrated organizationally. However, such reorganization unaccompanied by specific incentives to provide integrated supply and demand information with the express purpose of generating economically efficient allocations of manpower resources will likely entail little or no change in the current decisionmaking process.

It is, then, within OSD's role to provide the services with adequate guidance in making manpower allocations consistent with the goals and objectives determined for the force as a whole, including the objective of making allocations of manpower resources that are economically efficient. To the extent that this particular objective plays a role in overall defense policy objectives, incentives to expand capability for making economically efficient allocations of manpower resources should also be provided.

Appendix A

BACKGROUND AND DESCRIPTION OF THE
ENLISTED UTILIZATION SURVEY

The research for which the Enlisted Utilization Survey data base was generated centered on an assessment of the efficient amount of technical training for specific military occupational specialties.[1] The specific approach adopted involved estimating the costs of formal training (faculty and student salaries, supplies, etc.) and its benefits (i.e., improvements in trainees' on-the-job performance) in order to determine the effects of training variations on net training costs.

Several features of the specific analysis plan had major implications for the exact method of data collection. One was the necessity to construct productivity profiles for an individual's entire first term of service after completion of initial specialty training, since it was assumed that differences in training would manifest themselves in terms of enhanced on-the-job performance, and that these differences would persist over time. The estimates of productivity for individuals exposed to different lengths of training needed to relate to an individual's entire first term experience. For individuals who were serving at their first duty station, supervisors were asked to estimate what the individual's productivity was when he first joined the unit and what it was expected to be in the future. However, if the individual had served at other duty stations before arriving at his current unit, it was only possible to construct a complete profile by tracking down and surveying supervisors at the prior duty stations. Since that would have been expensive and time consuming, and success was quite uncertain, the only feasible method of constructing complete profiles was to limit the sample of individuals to persons who were currently serving at their first duty station.

It also seemed important to obtain ratings for specific individuals. These provided a basis for controlling for personal characteristics and thus a great deal of analytic flexibility in terms of empirically determining relevant categories of labor based on differences in experience. Moreover, estimates of the typical trainee do not necessarily reflect the productivity of the average trainee. Therefore, although we do feel it is useful to have estimates for the typical trainee, this research concentrated on estimating productivity for specific individuals.

Because of the size and scope of the planned research data it was not feasible to collect data through in-person interviews. The research was limited to data available in the service personnel files or that could be collected through mail surveys. The need to obtain ratings on specific individuals and the limitation of data retrieval, along with the fact that there is generally little formal information on the supervisor-trainee relationship included in the personnel files, dictated the design of the data collection plan.

This design involved four major steps. First, a set of specialties to be included in the study was selected. Second, using service personnel files, a set of individuals were identified who appeared to be in their first term of service and serving at their

---

[1] For a basic outline of the research program see Albrecht and Gay (1977).

first duty station. Third, these persons were sent a mail survey designed with three basic objectives: (1) identification of the trainee's primary supervisors, (2) verification of his suitability for inclusion in the study, and (3) collection of background information not included in the service record. Although the second and third objectives were important, the key element of the initial survey was the identification of the individual's supervisors. Responses from the survey of trainees were used to construct a mailing list and survey forms for surveying supervisors to elicit ratings of the individuals responding to the trainee questionnaire.

Compilation of the mailing list involved rearranging information provided by responding trainees. Specifically, for each military unit containing responding trainees, a list was made containing the names of each supervisor identified by a responding trainee and the names of all trainees who identified this individual as one of their supervisors. A copy of the supervisor survey form was then compiled for each supervisor including rating sheets for each of the specific individuals who named this supervisor as his own. Thus, the supervisor survey instrument's length varied depending on the number of trainees under his supervision.

The specific form of the supervisor survey contained three parts: (1) questions about the general conduct of on-the-job training in the unit and an explanation of the concept of productivity as it was used in the survey; (2) a set of questions pertaining to the utilization, performance, and attitudes of specific trainees who had identified this individual as one of his supervisors; (3) a section in which the supervisor was asked to rate the "typical trainee" at various points of a first term of service. These then are the basic mechanics of the Enlisted Utilization Survey. At this point it will be useful to go into more detail regarding the sample in terms of the selection of occupational specialties, the characteristics of the trainee and supervisory surveys, and the specific form of the measure of productivity utilized in this research. It should be mentioned that the following discussion applies equally to the samples from the Army, Navy, and Air Force included in the survey, but for the purposes of the actual productivity analysis we will restrict our consideration of the data base to the set of Air Force occupational specialties included in the sample.

SELECTION OF SPECIALTIES

The selection of specialties for inclusion in the on-the-job training study was, of course, one of the very important aspects of the research effort. Four criteria were used in determining the specialties to include in the study: (1) variations in the amount of training, (2) a large total cost of training, (3) a large number of potential cases for analysis, and (4) representation of the entire range of military occupational skills.

For the purposes of the on-the-job training study, the most important consideration in selecting specialties was that a potential for analyzing the effects of different amounts of initial specialty training exist. In this regard three types of training variation are represented in the sample: (1) variations within a service, for example the category 'B' specialties in the Air Force where some trainees receive formal training in an occupation while others receive only on-the-job training, (2) intertemporal changes in the length of specialty training within a service, and (3) differences in training practices among the services.

TOTAL TRAINING COST

Another important consideration in selecting specialties was the total annual cost of initial specialty training. The intention was to focus on those specialties where potential savings from improving the economic efficiency of training were greatest, and hence, those were likely to be specialties in which current outlays for training are greatest. Annual outlay for initial specialty training can be large either because the cost per trainee is relatively great or because large numbers of individuals are trained each year. It was, however, much easier to identify potential cases for the study in the latter category than in the former.

POTENTIAL SAMPLE SIZE

The third criterion that was employed in selecting specialties in the training study, potential sample size, was an important consideration for a number of reasons, since several aspects of the study design resulted in the need for sample sizes within each specialty that might, at first glance, seem quite large. These were related either to the planned method of analysis or the way in which data were to be collected. As previously noted, these plans called for constructing productivity profiles for specific individuals over their entire first term of service, and this required that the sample be composed of first term enlisted personnel serving at their first duty station. However, available data bases (i.e. service personnel records) do not provide information on the number of previous duty assignments. Therefore, our sample sizes had to allow for the fact that some fraction of the cases collected would be unusable because the data would pertain to individuals not serving at their first duty station. (Trainees were asked on the trainee survey whether they were serving at their first duty station and if not, how long they had served at other duty stations.) Moreover, the fraction of cases lost in this way could not be reliably estimated in advance. The other way in which planned methods of analysis affect the sample size involved controlling for differences among supervisors in the way in which they rate individuals. A pilot study and subsequent research indicated that controlling for such differences was very important and, further, that one effective way of doing so was to use a set of ratings from each supervisor to estimate simultaneously the supervisor's rating system and the effects of personal attributes on performance. Because two degrees of freedom are used in estimating each supervisory rating system, an effective sample of 100 cases may require as many as 300 useful ratings.[2]

The method of data collection also imposed constraints on the sample size. As previously noted, the data collection procedures involved a pair of sequential surveys—one to trainees, the other to their supervisors. It was obvious from the nature

---

[2] In addition to imposing limitations on total sample size, this constraint resulted in the exclusion of some specialties in which there were large numbers of individuals but they were distributed across a very large number of units such that the probability of finding a sufficient number of cases where supervisors rated three or more trainees (a necessary condition for using the Cooper-Nelson (1976, p. 13) methodology) was deemed to be too low to justify inclusion. However, substantial fieldwork indicated that when work units are small there tends to be an unusually high amount of heterogeneity in job tasks within the specialty, in which case it would probably not be wise to include the specialty for this reason alone. The most important exclusion on these grounds was that of clerical personnel in each of the services.

of this process that the number of usable productivity ratings would be affected by several factors that could only be roughly estimated at the time the research was planned. These included (1) the number of trainees responding to the first survey, (2) the average number of supervisors named by responding trainees, and (3) the number of supervisors responding to the supervisor survey. The number of responding trainees and supervisors is dependent on both the response rate among individuals actually receiving questionnaires, and imperfections in the ways trainees identified supervisors (i.e., misspelling, incorrect first names, incorrect ranks, etc.) were difficult to estimate in advance. Since an unexpectedly poor result at any of the three stages mentioned above could render a sample too small to be useful, these considerations led to the adoption of a conservative approach for evaluating potential sample sizes.

REPRESENTATION OF THE ENTIRE SERVICE

In addition to the previously mentioned criteria that apply to individual specialties, there was concern that, to the extent possible, the set of selected specialties should provide a representative picture of the entire service. There are two aspects of this concern. First, there was a desire with respect to the training study that the mix of selected specialties represent the entire range of technical difficulty in each service, since this would provide a basis for judging the pattern of cost across the full range of occupations and hence for estimating service-wide levels of net training costs.

The second reason for concern with service-wide representativeness is that there are certain specialties in each service that are so large and important that they must be included in the sample to provide a comprehensive picture of the service.

In addition, there were extenuating factors that were responsible for the inclusion in the sample of certain occupations—for example, the integrated avionics technicians in the Air Force (AFSC's 326X0, 326X1 and 326X2). These are recently established specialties in which the Air Force has had substantial difficulty providing trained manpower. They were included in the sample at least in part to take advantage of complementarities between this research and a separate study of the 326 career field being conducted at Rand under Air Force sponsorship.[3]

Although the above-mentioned criteria for selecting specialties were constructed largely with regard to the requirements of the training study, they are, in fact, also quite reasonable criteria for selecting specialties with respect to an analysis of the distribution of enlisted personnel by length of service. Assuming that a data collection plan for a study of the first term/career mix would be subject to similar constraints regarding the need to sample occupational specialties, the criteria of training cost, large potential sample size, and representativeness of the entire service would be a reasonable set upon which to base the selection of specialties for such an analysis. Training cost considerations are important since large training costs are likely to be associated with high skill occupations and, in turn, with occupations which, in all likelihood, experience difficulty in retaining qualified specialists beyond a first term. Considerations of potential sample size provide, at

---

[3] See Nelson, Gay, and Roll (1974).

least, a crude discriminator among occupations which, although large in terms of total numbers, are actually present in the field in small detachments for which the likely consolidations induced by a smaller more senior force would be difficult to achieve. Finally, considerations of representativeness ensure that the sample will reflect occupations both at the high and low end of the skill spectrum where differences in the efficient mixes are likely to be most apparent. Thus, although these specific criteria were designed to satisfy the requirements of the training study, they also provide a good basis for selection given the requirements of an analysis of efficient experience mixes.

SAMPLE OF SPECIALTIES

Table A.1 presents a list of the 58 military occupational specialties chosen on the basis of the criteria just discussed. In Table A.1 the specialties have been grouped by our view of the technical difficulty of the job tasks into high, medium, and low skill specialties. This grouping is not, of course, essential to the detailed analysis to be undertaken since that analysis will be done by a specialty-by-specialty basis, but it is helpful both in forming an overall view of the set of specialties and for certain very broad uses of the data set.

Although the number of specialties included in the sample is relatively small, it represents a large proportion of the total enlisted force. Members of the 58 specialties included in the study represent about 34 percent of the total enlisted force in the Army, Navy, and Air Force. They represent 24 percent of the Army, 55 percent of the Navy, and 25 percent of the Air Force. The reason such a large percentage of the total force is contained in this set of specialties is, of course, that the selection criteria were such that large specialties tended to be selected.

As can be seen from Table A.1, the range of specialties included in the sample is quite broad. Occupations in the sample include both cooks and vehicle operators, as well as cryptographic equipment repairmen and nuclear propulsion plant operators. This range of specialties provides an opportunity to assess the experience mix issue across the entire occupational spectrum and, thereby, to begin to address the issue on a force-wide basis.

Table A.1

SET OF SPECIALTIES

High Skill Specialties

Army		Navy		Air Force	
MOS[a]	Job Title	Rating/NEC[b]	Job Title	AFSC[c]	Job Title
26L [d]	Tactical Microwave Systems Repairman	AE 8325	Jet Aircraft Electrical Systems Repairman (F-4)	304X4	Ground Radio Repairman
26V	Strategic Microwave Systems Repairman			306X0	Electronic Communications and Cryptographic Equipment Systems Repairman
31E	Field Radio Repairman	AE 8327	Jet Aircraft Electrical Systems Repairman (A-7)		
31S	Field General Cryptographic Equipment Repairman				
31T	Field Systems Cryptographic Equipment Repairman	EM 3354	Submarine Nuclear Propulsion Plant Operator--Electrical	326X0	Avionic Aerospace Ground Equipment Specialist
32G	Fixed Cryptographic Equipment Repairman				
35L	Avionic Communication Equipment Repairman	ET	Electronics Technician	326X1	Integrated Avionic Component Specialist
35M	Avionic Navigation Equipment Repairman	ET 3353	Submarine Nuclear Propulsion Plant Operator--Reactor Control	326X2	Integrated Avionic Systems Specialist
35N	Avionic Flight Control Equipment Repairman	MM 3355	Submarine Nuclear Propulsion Plant Operator--Mechanical		

Medium Skill Specialties

Army		Navy		Air Force	
63H	Automotive Repairman	ADJ 8323	Jet Engine Mechanic (F-4)	421X3	Aerospace Ground Equipment Repairman
67N	UH-1 Helicopter Repairman	ADJ 8327	Jet Engine Mechanic (A-7)		
67U	CH-47 Helicopter Repairman	DT	Dental Technician	422X1	Aircraft Environmental Systems Repairman
67V	OH-6/OH-58 Helicopter Repairman	EM	Electrician's Mate		
73C	Finance Specialist	HM	Hospital Corpsman		
91B	Medical Specialist	RM	Radioman		
91E	Dental Specialist			431X1	Aircraft Maintenance Specialist
				542X0	Electrician
				543X0	Electrical Power Production Specialist
				671X3	Disbursement Accounting Specialist
				902X0	Medical Service Specialist
				981X0	Dental Specialist

Low Skill Specialties

Army		Navy		Air Force	
11B	Light Weapons Infantryman	AN	Airman		
11E	Armor Crewman	CS	Commissaryman (Mess Mgmt Spec.)	571X0	Fire Protection Specialist
12B	Combat Engineer	FN	Fireman		
13B	Field Artillery Crewman	MM	Machinist's Mate	622X0	Cook
51B	Carpenter	SN	Seaman	631X0	Fuels Specialist
64C	Motor Transport Operator			647X0	Material Facilities Specialist
94B	Food Service Specialist				

[a] Military Occupational Specialty.

[b] Naval Enlisted Classification.

[c] Air Force Specialty Code.

[d] Bracket indicates specialties that are to be combined for purposes of analysis.

COMPREHENSIVE TEST IN SURVEY INSTRUMENT

Specifically, each supervisor survey included the following section:

The following questions apply to individuals whose on-the-job performance should be familiar to you. One of the things we would like you to do is to rate their net contribution to unit production. Because the idea of net contribution to unit production is complicated, we have found that an example helps people understand what we mean.

Suppose an experienced specialist, *working alone*, can complete 10 jobs a day. If a trainee is assigned to work with him, the trainee will contribute to unit production by completing some jobs—say, 2 jobs per day. However, because the specialist must spend time supervising and instructing the trainee, his own production will drop. For example, he might now be able to complete only 5 jobs a day. In this case, the trainee's *NET* contribution to unit production is *negative* because the two people together are now completing *fewer* jobs than the experienced specialist was able to complete before the trainee was assigned to him. However, as the trainee gets more experienced, the combined production of the two men will increase. When they are able to produce 10 jobs a day, working together, the trainee's *NET* contribution to unit production will be *zero*, because the two men working together will be completing what the experienced specialist was completing before, working alone. When the supervisor and the trainee working together can complete *more* than 10 jobs a day, the trainee's *NET* contribution to unit production will be *positive*.

The pictures below illustrate another example:

The experienced cook can bake 15 pies a day when he works alone. When a trainee is assigned to work with him the cook bakes only 8 pies a day and the trainee bakes 3 pies a day.

TEST 67   1.   Would you say that the trainee's *NET CONTRIBUTION TO UNIT PRODUCTION* at this time is : (CHECK ONE)

    ( ) 1.   NEGATIVE

    ( ) 2.   ZERO

    ( ) 3.   POSITIVE

In the following questions you will be asked to estimate individuals' *NET CON-TRIBUTION TO UNIT PRODUCTION*. We ask that you assume each individual will serve at least 4 years and remain in this shop or section.

We realize that in many cases it will be difficult to give precise answers, but give the best estimates you can.

Once initial editing criteria were imposed on the responses, over 85 percent of the Air Force respondents correctly answered the above question.

Appendix C

COST ELEMENTS

This appendix is designed to provide a detailed discussion of the basic costing methodology presented in Section V. To reiterate, the basic costing technique is average marginal cost for enlisted personnel with 0-4 years of service (first term) and 5 or more years of service (career) computed as an average value over each of the years of service. The specific elements of cost contained in these estimates include (1) the basic pay, (2) allowances for quarters and subsistence, (3) miscellaneous cost elements, i.e., medical costs, commissary and exchange privileges etc., (4) training, both basic and advanced, and retirement. Each of these elements is described below.

Basic Pay

The basic pay element of cost estimated for each year of service reflects the basic pay rates as of October 1, 1977, weighted by the proportion of individuals serving in each pay grade at each year of service point. [SOURCE: OASD (MRA&L) (MPP)]

Allowance for Quarters and Subsistence

The allowance cost estimates for each year of service reflect the basic allowance for quarters and subsistence as of October 1, 1977, weighted by pay grade and dependency status within each year of service. [SOURCE: MRA&L (MPP)]

Support Costs

The support cost element reflects estimates of the per man cost of such miscellaneous and overhead costs as medical costs, commissary and exchange, recreation, and welfare by pay grade. These values by grade are weighted by the proportion of individuals serving in each pay grade at each year of service point.

[SOURCE: *Average Cost of Military and Civilian Manpower in the Department of Defense*, December 1977, Office of the Assistant Secretary of Defense (Comptroller).]

Retirement

Retirement costs are estimated as the present value of the retirement liability at the point of retirement evaluated at an 8 percent discount rate over 30 years of post service benefit and weighted by the distribution of personnel by pay grade at the point of retirement.

Specifically, an annual retirement benefit is computed as

$$R = \sum_{i=1}^{9} \gamma_i \; BP_i/2 \, ,$$

where γ_i reflects the proportion of individuals in the ith pay grade at the point of retirement, and BP_i reflects the value of basic pay for the ith pay grade at the point of retirement.

This annual retirement benefit, R, is then discounted over 30 years of past service benefit weighted in each year by the conditional probability of living that additional year. Thus, the present value of the retirement benefit at the point of retirement equals

$$PDVR = R \sum_{t=1}^{30} \phi_t \, (1 + i)^{-t} ,$$

where $i = .08$ and ϕ_t is the probability of surviving until the t-th year after retirement. To provide an example, assuming a 20 year retirement, the present value of the annuity at 20 years is equal to \$60,641.28.

Table C.1 summarizes these cost elements for each of the 30 years of service.

Table C.1

PAY AND ALLOWANCE COSTS

Year of Service	Basic Pay	Basic Allowance for Quarters & Subsistence	Miscellaneous & Support	Retirement	Total
1	5069	1229	2657		8955
2	5519	1404	2598		9521
3	6014	1564	3097		10675
4	6492	1716	3245		11453
5	7026	1886	3418	3790	16120
6	7110	1977	3418	3790	16295
7	7637	2044	3418	3790	16889
8	7762	2099	3418	3790	17069
9	8195	2162	3547	3790	17694
10	8305	2203	3547	3790	17845
11	8779	2262	3547	3790	18379
12	8898	2292	3547	3790	18531
13	9435	2234	3653	3790	19112
14	9625	2387	3653	3790	19455
15	10105	2421	3653	3790	19969
16	10252	2452	3653	3790	20147
17	10727	2489	3813	3790	20819
18	10908	2523	3813	3790	21034
19	11316	2550	3813	3790	21449
20	11496	2578	3813	3790	21667
21	12148	2655	3979	3790	22572
22	12466	2700	3979	3790	22935
23	13460	2738	3979	3790	23967
24	13919	2796	3979	3790	24484
25	14527	2880	4149	3790	25346
26	14732	2904	4149	3790	25575
27	16620	2940	4149	3790	27499
28	16936	2988	4149	3790	27863
29	17235	3028	4149	3790	28202
30	17260	3031	4149	3790	28230

SOURCE: OASD (MRA&L), OASD (Comptroller)

BIBLIOGRAPHY

Albrecht, M. J., and R. Gay, *Enlisted Specialty Training and the Performance of First Term Enlisted Personnel*, The Rand Corporation, R-2191-ARPA, April 1977.

Allen, R., *Mathematical Analysis for Economists*, St. Martin's Press, New York, 1964.

K. Arrow, H. Chenery, B. Minhas, and R. Solow, "Capital-Labor Substitution and Economic Efficiency," *Review of Economics and Statistics*, Vol. 43, August 1961, pp. 225-250.

"Average Cost of Military and Civilian Manpower in the Department of Defense," Office of the Assistant Secretary of Defense (Comptroller), December 1977.

Bowles, S., "Aggregation of Labor Inputs in the Economics of Growth and Planning: Experiments with a Two-Level CES Function," *Journal of Political Economy*, Vol. 78, February 1970.

Cooper, R.V.L., *Military Manpower and the All-Volunteer Force*, The Rand Corporation, R-1450-ARPA, September 1977.

——, and G. Nelson, *Analytic Methods for Adjusting Subjective Rating Schemes*, The Rand Corporation, R-1685-ARPA, June 1976.

Dougherty, C., "Estimates of Labor Aggregation Functions," *Economic Development Reports*, The Center for International Affairs, Harvard University, Cambridge, Mass., 1971.

B-K Dynamics, Inc., *Development of a Utility Measure for Manpower Planning*, TR-3-177, February 28, 1973.

Enns, J. H., *Effect of the Variable Reenlistment Bonus on Reenlistment Rates: Empirical Rates for FY 1971*, The Rand Corporation, R-1502-ARPA, June 1975.

Fisher, A. C., "The Cost of the Draft and the Cost of Ending the Draft," *American Economic Review*, Vol. LIX, No. 3, June 1969.

Fisher, F., "U.S. Experience: Recent INS Study," in J. Wolfe (ed.), *The Armed Services and Society*, University of Edinburgh Press, 1970.

——, "The Existence of Aggregate Production Functions," *Econometrica*, Vol. 37, No. 4, 1969.

Gates, Thomas, et al., *Studies Prepared for the President's Commission on All-Volunteer Armed Force, Part II, Supply of Personnel to the Military*, Vol. I, November 1970.

Gay, R. M., *Estimating the Cost of On-the-Job Training in Military Occupations: A Methodology and Pilot Study*, The Rand Corporation, R-1351-ARPA, April 1974.

Green, J., *Aggregation in Economic Analysis: An Introductory Survey*, Princeton University Press, Princeton, New Jersey, 1964.

Griliches, Z., "Specification Bias in Estimates of Production Functions," *Journal of Farm Economics*, Vol. 39, 1957, pp. 8-20.

Grissmer, D. W., J. D. Pearson, and R. Szymanski, *Evaluation of the Modern Volunteer Armed Program*, Research Analysis Corporation, November 1972.

Henderson, J., and R. Quandt, *Microeconomic Theory*, 2d ed., McGraw Hill, New York, 1971.

Hitch, Charles, "Suboptimization in Operations Problems," *Journal of the Operations Research Society of America*, May 1953, pp. 87-99.

Horowitz, S., and A. Sherman, "Maintenance Personnel Effectiveness in the Navy," Center for Naval Analysis, Professional Paper No. 143, January 1976.

Jaquette, D. L., and G. R. Nelson, *The Implications of Manpower Supply and Productivity for the Pay and Composition of the Military Force: An Optimization Model*, The Rand Corporation, R-1451-ARPA, July 1974.

——, G. R. Nelson, and R. J. Smith, *An Analytic Review of Personnel Models in the Department of Defense*, The Rand Corporation, R-1920-ARPA, September 1977.

Leontief, Wassily, "Introduction to a Theory of the Internal Structure of Functional Relationships," *Econometrica*, Vol. 15, No. 4, October 1947, pp. 361-373.

Munch, P., *A Dynamic Model for Optimum Bonus Management*, The Rand Corporation, R-1940-ARPA, January 1977.

Nelson, G., R. Gay, and C. Roll, Jr., *Manpower Cost Reduction in Electronics Maintenance: Framework and Recommendations*, The Rand Corporation, R-1483-ARPA, July 1974.

Sato, K., "A Two-Level Constant Elasticity of Substitution Production Function," *Review of Economic Studies*, Vol. 34, April 1967.

Scifers, L. V., "A Productivity Analysis of Air Reserve Force Flying Units," unpublished dissertation, the Rand Graduate Institute, August 1974.

Smith, G., "Occupational Pay Differentials for Military Technicians," unpublished dissertation, Columbia University, 1964.

Vineberg, R., and E. Taylor, *Performance in Four Army Jobs by Men at Different Aptitude (AFQT) Levels: 3. The Relationships of AFQT and Job Experience to Job Performance*, HumRRO, Technical Report 72-22, August 1972.